Prayers to the Great Creator

By Julia Cameron

Prayers to the Great Creator

*Prayers and Declarations
for a Meaningful Life*

JULIA CAMERON

JEREMY P. TARCHER/PENGUIN
a member of Penguin Group (USA) Inc.
New York

JEREMY P. TARCHER/PENGUIN
Published by the Penguin Group
Penguin Group (USA) Inc., 375 Hudson Street, New York, New York 10014, USA •
Penguin Group (Canada), 90 Eglinton Avenue East, Suite 700, Toronto, Ontario
M4P 2Y3, Canada (a division of Pearson Canada Inc.) • Penguin Books Ltd,
80 Strand, London WC2R 0RL, England • Penguin Ireland, 25 St Stephen's Green,
Dublin 2, Ireland (a division of Penguin Books Ltd) • Penguin Group (Australia),
250 Camberwell Road, Camberwell, Victoria 3124, Australia (a division of Pearson
Australia Group Pty Ltd) • Penguin Books India Pvt Ltd, 11 Community Centre,
Panchsheel Park, New Delhi–110 017, India • Penguin Group (NZ), 67 Apollo
Drive, Rosedale, North Shore 0632, New Zealand (a division of Pearson
New Zealand Ltd) • Penguin Books (South Africa) (Pty) Ltd, 24 Sturdee Avenue,
Rosebank, Johannesburg 2196, South Africa

Penguin Books Ltd, Registered Offices:
80 Strand, London WC2R 0RL, England

Most Tarcher/Penguin books are available at special quantity discounts for bulk
purchase for sales promotions, premiums, fund-raising, and educational needs.
Special books or book excerpts also can be created to fit specific needs.
For details, write Penguin Group (USA) Inc. Special Markets,
375 Hudson Street, New York, NY 10014.

Library of Congress Cataloging-in-Publication Data

Cameron, Julia.
Prayers to the Great Creator : prayers and declarations for
a meaningful life / Julia Cameron.
p.   cm.
ISBN 978-1-58542-682-9
1. Meditations   2. Self-actualization (Psychology)—Religious aspects—
Meditations.   I. Cameron, Julia. Heart steps.   II. Cameron, Julia. Blessings.
III. Cameron, Julia. Transitions.   IV. Cameron, Julia. Answered prayers.   V. Title.
BL624.2.C352   2008   2008025921
204'.33—dc22

Printed in the United States of America
1   3   5   7   9   10   8   6   4   2

Book design by Amanda Dewey and Claire Naylon Vaccaro

While the author has made every effort to provide accurate telephone numbers and
Internet addresses at the time of publication, neither the publisher nor the author
assumes any responsibility for errors, or for changes that occur after publication.
Further, the publisher does not have any control over and does not assume any
responsibility for author or third-party websites or their content.

CONTENTS

PREFACE

It is a chill, gray spring day, and yet forsythia are blooming, daffodils are out, and magnolia trees bear heavy buds, promising that they, too, will bloom again soon. Even in Manhattan, nature is a determined optimist. Hope is in the air. It is as though every bush and twig has said a prayer and is unfurling on blind faith. Despite the chill, spring prevails. Tutored by nature, we, too, can turn our hearts to hope. Using prayer, we can consciously connect to what Dylan Thomas called, "the force that through the green fuse drives the flower." Like the natural world, we can say "yes" to God.

Prayer is the doorway to higher realms. When we pray, we practice swinging the door open. We forge a connection to the Great Creator. We voice an "allelujah" that sparks answering "allelujahs." It is God's desire to have a conversation with each of us. When we pray, we enter a dialogue with the divine. Even in times of great despair, when we feel ourselves speaking into a void, no prayer goes unanswered.

There are many forms of prayer. As a practice, it is as individual as we ourselves. There are prayers of celebration, gratitude, acceptance, and petition, to name but a few. The prayers collected in this volume reflect many different moods and colors. They have been written over a decade's time, and reflect my own spiritual journey.

I have written these prayers as a response to many situations. They reflect my ongoing request for conscious contact with the Great Creator. It is my belief that God responds to each of us individually. The prayers I have written serve as a bridge from our regular, daily human consciousness to the divine. I believe that all prayers are filled with grace—that mysterious force which transforms our consciousness from barren to verdant. It is one of the ongoing ironies of the spiritual life that as we pray for others, we reap the benefit of prayer ourselves. It is my hope that this modest book will serve you as both guide and blueprint. I have written prayers which may in turn catalyze prayers of your own.

Use this volume as a spiritual stepping stone: each of the four books, now gathered as a bouquet, has a distinctive fragrance. "Heart Steps" celebrates our creative nature. "Blessings" offers prayers of gratitude. "Transitions" invokes grace in difficult passages, and finally, "Answered Prayers" gives us a hint of the care and compassion with which God regards his creatures.

Some of you may work through the book systematically; others may find wisdom in opening to a random page. No matter how you choose to use this volume, you will feel a heightened spiritual contact. That is the fruit of prayer.

In writing these prayers, I found myself more and more closely aligned with the Great Creator. Optimism and faith were among the gifts I received. May you find these gifts at your doorstep.

Heart Steps

Prayers and Declarations
for a Creative Life

To those who have gone before us

INTRODUCTION

This small book is intended as a journey, an exploration into spiritual realms. I invite you to undertake it in the spirit of scientific inquiry. I ask you to experiment with these prayers and declarations and to record for yourself the results you observe in your life and in your consciousness.

Heart Steps is grounded in ancient spiritual tradition. You are asked to "speak the word." In other words, this book is intended not merely to be read, but to be read aloud. (For this reason, I have made an audiotape combining the words of this book with the powerful music of my creative partner, Tim Wheater.)

"In the beginning was the Word," Scripture tells us. The ancients sang the world into existence, Aboriginals believe. Ethiopians believe that the world and God Himself were created by God speaking His own name. In Hopi belief, it was Spider Woman who sang the world into existence—one word at a time. Indians believe, *"Nada Brahma: the world is sound."* As even this brief scan suggests, it is difficult to find a spiritual tradition that does not emphasize the creative power of the word. From the Lakota songs of North America to the song lines crossing Australia, spiritual seekers have always used language—sound—as a safe haven. It is a stairway to higher consciousness as well. I do not ask you to believe this. Instead, I ask you to experiment and see for yourself whether this is true.

The tone of these prayers may at first startle you. These are declarative prayers. They do not beseech divine help, they assume it. These are not the prayers of a sinful, fallen nature begging for release. These are prayers spoken with confidence as children of the Universe. These prayers claim our birthright. They acknowledge and expand our co-creative bond with a power greater than ourselves. They are not the prayers of exile. They are the prayers of reunion, renewal, and return. God is not "dead." God is not absent from our world. Our consciousness of God is what is missing. "Conscious contact" is what these prayers are all about.

In 1979, composer Billy May gave me a small book of prayers, *Creative Ideas*, by Dr. Ernest Holmes.

"These have worked for me," Billy said.

"Worked?"

"They clear the way."

At the time we were talking, I was newly sober and wondering just how to "let" myself be creative without alcohol as a crutch or a reward.

"I think of it like this," Billy continued. "If you're working on a project and you have a hundred creative horses, you want all of them with you. Now, if thirty of your horses are worried about money, and thirty of your horses are worried about the way the project will be received, you only have another forty to do the creative work at hand. These prayers help you to gather your horses."

With that, he handed me the tiny book.

What a revolution that tiny book caused in my life and in my thinking! I had never read prayers like those, prayers spoken with the confident assurance that God, or "Mind," was deeply, personally interested and interactive in our lives—if we would just speak the word that opened the door that opens the heart.

From 1979 until now, I have worked with—and played with—the power of the positive word. I have found the techniques in this book not merely enlivening or empowering, but actually "healing." They have given me a creative life.

Julia Cameron

The power of the word
is real whether or not
you are conscious of it.

Your own words are the
bricks and mortar of the
dreams you want to realize.
Behind every word flows energy.

SONIA CHOQUETTE

THE UNIVERSE RESPONDS TO MY DREAMS AND NEEDS

There is a unity flowing through all things. This unity is responsive to our needs. Unity responds and reacts to our positive spoken word. We are co-creative beings working with—and within—a larger whole. We embrace and contain this Source, which embraces and contains us. Drawing upon this Inner Source, we have an unlimited supply.

Through the act of affirmative
prayer the limitless resources
of the Spirit are at my command.
The power of the Infinite
is at my disposal.

ERNEST HOLMES

☙

I HAVE THE POWER TO
RECEIVE GREAT ABUNDANCE

I open myself to a more abundant flow. I source myself in the Universe and recognize that the Universe is unlimited in its abundance. I allow myself to receive abundance as a show of the power of God working through me. I allow my life to be made abundant and rich as an example that the power of God can make life abundant and rich. I accept increased flow as proof of God's power. I am receptive soil for God's gardening hands.

I myself do nothing. The Holy Spirit
accomplishes all through me.

WILLIAM BLAKE

Cᕤ

THE DREAMS OF MY HEART
ARE THE DREAMS OF
THE UNIVERSE DREAMING
THROUGH ME

I am a gate for God to accomplish great things. Through me and with me, new Life enters the world. I am a portal, an entryway for the grace and power of God to show themselves in the world. As I move toward my fulfillment, God moves toward fulfillment. I am a particle and an article of faith. As I accept the power of God within me, I manifest that power in the world. What I desire is good and what I make is good. My creative nature brings blessings to me and to my world.

Our worst fear is not that we are
inadequate, our deepest fear is that
we are powerful beyond measure.

NELSON MANDELA

☙

THE GREAT CREATOR
CREATES THROUGH ME

We are ourselves creations. We are meant to continue creativity by being creative ourselves. This is the God-force extending itself through us. Creativity is God's gift to us. Using creativity is our gift back to God. It is the natural extension of our creative nature to manifest our dreams. Our dreams come from a divine source. Moving in the direction of our dreams moves us toward our divinity.

THE UNIVERSE WATCHES
OVER ME WITH CARE

I am a beloved child of God. The Universe is my home. I am safe and protected in all places, at all times. There is no harm or danger in which my well-being is not provided for. I accept guidance, guardianship in all areas of my life. There is no venture I undertake, no plan or project I conceive which is not shepherded safely. I consciously and daily invoke the protective guidance of God. I receive this guidance within and from people and situations I encounter. I am gently, safely led.

Man can learn nothing except
by going from the known
to the unknown.

CLAUDE BERNARD

❧

I AM LUMINOUS AND SAFE
IN MY VULNERABILITY

Life requires vulnerability. I treat myself gently and allow myself to be vulnerable. I accept myself as I am today without the need for perfection. I allow myself the freedom to learn without grandiose expectations. I am a living being. I allow my life to flow more broadly across the plain of experience. I allow my life to rest in the sun of self-acceptance.

There are unknown forces within nature;
when we give ourselves wholly to her,
without reserve, she leads them to us;
she shows us those forms which
our watching eyes do not see,
which our intelligence does not
understand or suspect.

AUGUSTE RODIN

ALL CREATURES ARE
DIVINE IN ORIGIN

All creatures are my brothers and sisters. All life exists in God. There is no hierarchy, only harmony. There is a right place for each of us. Each is an important part of the web of Life. Not one of us is dispensable. All are valued. All are important. I am a valued and important part of the web of Life. The web of Life is a valued and important part of me.

༚

ALL OF LIFE IS
MY MENTOR

I honor the wisdom of Life. I learn from Life in all its forms.
The tree teaches me. The sparrow and the wren sing my song.
I am open to the lessons Life brings to me from the earth. I learn
from the wind, from the sun, from the small flowers, and from
the stars. I walk without arrogance. I learn from all I encounter. I
open my mind and my heart to the guidance and love that come
to me from the natural world.

All is procession; the
universe is a procession
With measured and beautiful motion.

WALT WHITMAN

⁂

THOSE WHO LOVE ME
COME TO MY SIDE

As I ask for loving companions on my journey, I am led
heart to heart and hand to hand to a friendlier world. As I
extend my heart and my hand, the world meets me with open
arms. As I reach for my wisdom and my compassion to aid others,
others respond to me in kind. I am not alone. I am not unseen, unheard, a stranger in the world. As I hold myself a friend among
friends, friendship finds me. As I hold myself a lover of Life, Life
responds to me with love. In all times of sorrow and anxiety, I
comfort myself through comforting the world. Through cherishing Life, I allow Life to cherish me.

Man cannot live without mystery.
He has a great need of it.

❦

I LOVE WITH DIVINE
ENERGY AND WISDOM

The face of love is variable. I am able to love without demanding that my relationships assume the structures and forms I might choose for them. My love is fluid, flexible, committed, creative. My love allows people and events to unfold as they need. My love is not controlling. It does not dictate or demand. My love allows those I love the freedom to assume the forms most true to them. I release all those I love from my preconceptions of their path. I allow them the dignity of self-definition while I offer them a constant love that is ever variable in shape.

&

I DRAW TO ME TRUE LOVE

I draw to myself my right partner, the soul whose love serves my soul's highest potential, the soul whom my soul enhances to highest potential. I draw this partner to me freely and lovingly as I am drawn to this partner. I choose and am chosen out of pure love, pure respect, and pure liberty. I attract one who attracts me equally. I seek and am found. We are a match made in heaven to better this earth.

To me the concept of the "Beloved"

conveys not just a nice, cozy,

warm relationship with God,

but one that is joyous, uplifting

and exhilarating because it is

a recognition of who I am.

NINA YFIRY

☙

I LOVE AND AM LOVED
FULLY AND FREELY

My desire to love and be loved is a healthy part of my human nature. Giving and receiving love are as natural as breathing out and breathing in. I breathe in the love I need from Source, which is within me and all around me. I breathe out the love others need. I am nurtured both by giving and by receiving. I freely allow others to love me. I myself freely love others.

I believe the lasting revolution
comes from deep changes in ourselves
which influence our collective life.

ANAÏS NIN

❧

MY HEART EXPLORES
THE WORLD WITH WONDER

Life is an adventure. I am an explorer. The world I experience lies within me. The adventures I undertake are within me as well as in the world. I am wonderful and mysterious. I have depths and heights which are beautiful and expansive. As the world is magnificent, so am I. We are one Life, one substance, one growth moving toward fuller love. As I open my heart to the adventure of living, my horizons broaden and my path becomes clear.

The idea is like a blueprint,
it creates an image of the form,
which then magnetizes and guides
the physical energy to flow into that
form and eventually manifests
it on the physical plane.

I AM A MAGNET FOR GOOD

I attract to myself what I need to grow and expand. As a plant attracts physical nutrients, I attract spiritual nutrients. I attract people, things, and experiences which enhance my potential. I am a magnet for good. I draw to myself love, abundance, creativity, and opportunity. I radiate love, abundance, creativity, and opportunity for others.

The position of the artist is humble.
He is essentially a channel.

PIET MONDRIAN

☙

LIFE ADVANCES THROUGH
MY ATTITUDES AND ACTIONS

Life extends itself through Life. I am a channel for Life to expand and flourish. I am a branch reaching to the sun. As I reach my full potential, I aid and enhance all of Life. My good is good for everyone. My growth is growth for everyone. As I advance, we advance. The Universe moves through me. I move through the Universe. There is harmony, grace, and power in my unfolding.

One of the first things to do is learn
to accept, and to expect this Power to
flow through everything we do.

ERNEST HOLMES

෫

MY CREATIVITY
IS DIVINE IN ORIGIN,
HUMAN IN FORM

Life is energy, pure creative energy. This energy is the source of all I desire, all I need, all I want. When I call upon this source to supply me, I am freed from depending on people, institutions, and hierarchies. My good comes to me from all directions, from all quarters. No one person can block my good. No circumstance can circumvent me. There are ways and means for God to reach me beyond my imagining. I ask God directly to supply my needs. I listen for guidance and expect support in all I undertake.

Why should we all use our creative
power . . . ? Because there is nothing
that makes people so generous, joyful,
lively, bold and compassionate, so
indifferent to fighting and the
accumulation of objects and money.

BRENDA UELAND

☙

MY HEART IS RECEPTIVE TO THE PROMPTINGS OF SPIRIT

I am attentive to the guidance unfolding in my life. I am alert to promptings from within and without. I act in the world and I allow the world to act also in my affairs. I expect a responsive Universe to react and respond to me. As I become clear and focused for good, my world becomes clear and focused for good. I am a creator engaged in a creative relationship with the world within me and around me. As I create my inner world, my outer world responds in kind. As I establish peace, prosperity, and joy within my heart, these things are manifest in my outer reality.

It is in the knowledge of the
genuine conditions of our lives
that we must draw our strength to
live and our reasons for living.

SIMONE DE BEAUVOIR

☙

MY SOUL IS SUREFOOTED
ON ITS PATH

Balance is the key to my serenity. I attain balance by listening to my inner wisdom and to the wisdom of others. There is no situation in which I cannot find a point of balance. There is no circumstance in which I cannot find inner harmony. As I ask to be led into equilibrium and clarity, I will find that my answers come to me. I am wiser than I know, more capable of right action and attitudes than I yet believe. In every event, I seek the balance point of God's action through me.

All nature is alive, awake and
aware with the Divine Presence,
and everything in life responds
to the song of the heart.

ERNEST HOLMES

MINE IS AN
ADVENTUROUS HEART

I choose an expansive life. I choose adventure, freedom, self-expression. I choose self-definition, self-love, self-renewal. Life expands or contracts according to my expectations. I expect good and that is what I experience. Viewing the whole, I choose to be interconnected yet independent. I allow the God-force within me to open and enlarge my lens of perception and realm of action. My horizons stretch ever wider as I define my identity in terms of my divinity. I am an adventurer, an explorer, a dreamer whose dreams become true. I embrace the adventure of life. I have courage.

You must do the thing you
think you cannot do.

ELEANOR ROOSEVELT

Ↄ

THE UNIVERSE GIFTS
ME WITH COURAGE

I am courageous. I allow the Universe to strengthen and support me as I face difficult, demanding, and dangerous situations. I accept universal help, universal protection, universal guidance. I respond with calm bravery to perilous times, knowing the power of God works through me, so what have I to fear? God protects me. God surrounds me. God is within me. I am without fear.

No man is born into the world
whose work is not born with him.

JAMES RUSSELL LOWELL

ⳍ

MY GOOD IS POWERFUL
AND CANNOT BE STOPPED

There is no outer block to my highest good. No person, situation, event, or misfortune can block the flow of good to me. The flow of good is within me. All things work toward the good. As I allow love to come to me, I am fulfilling my true nature. I am listening to the voice within me which says, "Grow, blossom, this love is nutrition for your true nature." I accept love as I accept the sunshine, the moistening rain. It is natural. I need only receive it.

I know not what you believe in God, but I believe
He gave yearnings and longings to be filled,
and that He did not mean all
our time should be devoted to
feeding and clothing the body.

LUCY STONE

MY HEART IS CERTAIN
OF ITS GOOD

I am optimistic. I choose to believe and expect the emergence of the best. I enjoy the day I am given and I eagerly anticipate the future. I am alert to negative thinking and I do not allow it to cloud my perceptions. Knowing the unstoppable power of God, I am realistic about people and events but I am optimistic about positive outcomes, positive change. I invite actualizing grace to enter and act in all my affairs, alchemizing difficulty into opportunity.

Say yes to life, even though you know it will
devour you. Because among the obstacles
and, to be sure, the cruelties of life
are signs that we are on a primary
spiritual adventure (even though it seems
to be taking place in what we regard
as an unmistakably physical world).

STEPHEN LARSEN

☙

I AM LARGER
THAN MY PAIN

All loss is a doorway. All pain is an entrance. All suffering is a gate. The Universe is large enough to hold my pain and comfort me. I am small enough to be held and cherished, rocked and soothed. I am large enough to hold compassion, large enough to hold peace. I am united with all through my suffering and through my joy. I connect to my emotions and I connect to others through their emotions. I am both the mountain and the cloud. Circumstances vary, situations change, but I remain rooted in the soil of God. The Universe consoles me and makes me whole.

A wise man never loses
anything if he have himself.

Michel Eyquem de Montaigne

☙

MY DIGNITY IS SACRED
AND SELF-CONTAINED

I hold my value, honor, and dignity regardless of circumstances. I do not allow the thoughtless or unwarranted behavior of others to cause me to doubt or forget my own worth. In all times of stress and opposition, I ground myself by the spiritual truth that I am divinely sourced, protected, and cherished. I know and affirm that all things work toward my ultimate good through God's grace. I recognize there is no circumstance immune to the power of God. I ask divine intervention in my troublesome affairs. I expect and receive divine intervention and solution. I receive direct and active help.

If the world is to be healed
through human efforts, I am
convinced it will be by ordinary
people, people whose love for
this life is even greater than
their fear. People who can open
to the web of life that called us
into being, and who can rest in
the vitality of that larger body.

JOANNA MACY

THE UNIVERSE FUNDS ME
WITH STRENGTH

In times of adversity, I remember I am strong enough to meet the challenges of my life. I am equal to every situation, a match for every difficulty. Sourced in the power of the Universe, I allow that power to work through me. I meet calamity with strength. I have stamina. Rather than draw on limited resources, I draw on the infinite power within me that moves through me to accomplish its good. I am fueled by all the love, all the strength there is. Loving strength melts mountains. I am ever partnered and supplied by universal flow. Knowing this, I do not doubt my strength. I am strong and secure.

☙

MY SPIRIT
IS LARGE ENOUGH
FOR ANY CIRCUMSTANCE

I am enough. I have wisdom enough. I have faith enough. I know enough. I do not need to strive or strain. I do not need to reach or worry. I am enough. I allow the Universe to act through me. The Universe is more than enough. And so am I.

Undoubtedly, we become
what we envisage.
CLAUDE M. BRISTOL

❧

MY SOUL
IS RICH BEYOND
MY KNOWING

I honor the creator within me. I carry riches, jewels, and abundance. I have a bountiful heart. I am dowried by love, by compassion, by companionship. I act with generosity. I am sourced in God. All goodness flows to me and through me. There is no limit to what I can accomplish. I am the hand of Life flowing toward greater Life. My creations are the creations of the creator within me. I create with freedom and power. I create with bliss and excitement. Through me and in me, the powers of the Universe move to expansion. I am within that power, expanded by that power. It is within me and is expanded through me. As the Universe is powerful and good, so, too, am I.

Expect your every need to be met,
expect the answer to every problem,
expect abundance on every level,
expect to grow spiritually.

EILEEN CADDY

☙

GOD IS THE ROOT OF
MY ABUNDANT SECURITY

Sourced by the Universe, I am able to be generous. I am rooted in the wealth of God as a tree in rich soil. I share with others from God's unending abundance. As I share, I am replenished. There is no lack, no shortfall, only flow. I trust and affirm there is enough—more than enough—for all of us. As I share God's abundance, my flow increases. As I celebrate my increased flow, opportunities and occasions for still greater generosity appear to me, presenting themselves as opportunities for my extended faith. Trusting that I am a channel for universal flow, I allow good and abundance to move through me, prospering others and myself. As I prosper others, I am prospered in return.

☙

I AM PART
OF A GREATER WHOLE
AND IT IS A PART
OF ME

I open my mind and my heart to the plan of service which yields joy for me and others. I accept my guidance and direction as they unfold within me. I undertake actions which empower and embody my guidance. I release others from my agendas, trusting completely that the perfect people and events arise for me as I follow my own path.

Now join your hands and with
your hands your hearts.
WILLIAM SHAKESPEARE

ↁ

I CELEBRATE
THE FULFILLMENT OF
CREATIVE SERVICE

I find joy in service. I open my mind and my heart to the plan of service that brings the most joy to me and to others. I accept my guidance and direction as they unfold within me. Moved by my inner wisdom, I undertake actions which empower and embody my guidance. Moving forward as I am inwardly directed, I release others from my agendas, trusting completely that the perfect people and events will arise to meet me as I follow my path.

This we know: All things
are connected
like the blood which unites
one family.
All things are connected.
Whatever befalls the earth
befalls the sons of the earth.
Man did not weave the
web of life.
He is merely a strand of it.
Whatever he does to the web
He does to himself.

CHIEF SEATTLE

I EMBRACE THE
APPETITES OF LIFE

Life is tender and rapacious. Everything is fuel for further Life. Further growth. Nothing which I experience counts for nothing. Everything—all joy, all loss, all grief, all grace—is an ingredient in the greater self which I am building. I am not alone. All sense of loneliness is a forgetting. When I remember that I am a part of Life and Life is a part of me, I am comforted. I see my value. I experience my worth. I allow the Universe to touch me with compassion, to cradle me with love. I am held by the web of Life which I hold dear.

The song and the land are one.

BRUCE CHATWIN

❧

THE EARTH
AND I
ARE ONE LIFE

This earth is made from God. God is made from this earth. There is one substance, one nature, one energy which flows through all and is all. I am a part of this greater whole. This greater whole is a part of me. I am larger than I know.

A discovery is said to be an accident
meeting a prepared mind.
ALBERT SZENT-GYÖRGYI

☙

MY HEART OPENS
TO ALLOW
MY DEEPEST GOOD

Acceptance, openness, allowing are the keys to manifestation. I do not need to will my good. I need to accept my good. I do not need to will my being loved. I need only accept my being loved. I open my heart to accept and allow the good which I desire. I open my heart to accept and allow the love which I desire. I am in God and God is in me. As I yearn for God, I yearn for my own true nature. As I ask God to fulfill me, I ask that I fulfill myself. There is no distance, no need to please and cajole, whimper or manipulate. It is the pleasure of the entire Universe to expand as it desires. My desires are the desires of the Universe. They are fulfilled by the Universe acting through me, toward me.

We have been taught to believe
that negative equals realistic and
positive equals unrealistic.

SUSAN JEFFERS

❧

MY NOURISHMENT COMES
FROM MANY SOURCES

I open myself to abundance from all quarters. I open myself to nourishment and to love. I receive my good in many forms, through many people. I accept my good in all the multiple costumes and disguises which it may undertake. My good comes to me as people, as events and opportunities. My good comes to me as wise counsel, as friendship, as passion and delight. I honor my good by recognizing its many forms. I am grateful and attentive to the abundant good of Life.

*We will discover the nature of our
particular genius when we stop
trying to conform to our own or to
other people's models, learn to be
ourselves, and allow our natural
channel to open.*

SHAKTI GAWAIN

❧

LOYALTY IS MY GIFT
AND MY NATURE

I am loyal to myself and others. I am true to what I believe in and I am true to whom I believe in. My values are grounded in spiritual principles. I place principles before personalities. I do not shape my loyalties to fit convenience. The bedrock of my life is valuing what I know to be real and true. On this I stake all else: that each of us contains divinity, that each of us is worthy of respect, that each of us carries a birthright of dignity and honor. Knowing this, I find loyalty easy, even effortless. Grounded in my own divinity, I am true to what I know to be the truth.

We are the flow, we are the ebb.
We are the weavers; we are the web.

SHEKINAH MOUNTAINWATER

&

I CELEBRATE
THE COMMUNION OF
EQUAL HEARTS

I honor the equal wisdom of all souls. I listen for my own guidance and grant to all souls the same dignity. I trust that as I listen, I am properly led. I trust that as others listen, they, too, are led properly and perfectly for the highest good of all.

You must learn to be still in
the midst of activity and to be
vibrantly alive in repose.

INDIRA GANDHI

❧

MY TEMPERAMENT AND TEMPO ARE ATTUNED TO THE UNIVERSAL FLOW

I surrender my anxiety and my sense of urgency. I allow God to guide me in the pacing of my life. I open my heart to God's timing. I release my deadlines, agendas, and stridency to the gentle yet often swift pacing of God. As I open my heart to God's unfoldings, my heart attains peace. As I relax into God's timing, my heart contains comfort. As I allow God to set the tone and schedule of my days, I find myself in the right time and place, open and available to God's opportunities.

Taking a new step, uttering a new word
is what people fear most.

FYODOR DOSTOYEVSKY

❧

I EMBRACE
THE MOMENT

I am fluid and spontaneous. I react and respond openly and easily to the changing face of life. I am focused yet lighthearted. I bring joy and exuberance to my activities. I draw my energy from Life itself. I am an outlet for the energy of the Universe to promote change, growth, and expansion. As I expand and extend my goals and desires, my energies and stamina expand to encompass them. I fulfill my new potential. Knowing I am sourced in universal power, I respond to life with security, spontaneity, and delight. I am more than enough.

Today I live in the quiet
joyous expectation of good.

ERNEST HOLMES

❧

MY SOUL HAS PATIENCE
AND CONTAINMENT

I am patient. I am able to live with ambiguity. I am able to allow situations to evolve and alter. I am able to await outcomes. I tolerate quiet periods of non-knowing while solutions emerge and present themselves. I do not force solutions. I expect the successful working-out of difficulties and differences. My heart is wise. It knows when to act and when non-action is the action to take. I trust my patient heart. I trust the power of my containment.

Life shrinks or expands in
proportion to one's courage.

ANAÏS NIN

❧

DEATH IS A DOOR TO
FURTHER LIFE

Life intends Life. There is no death that is not another life beginning. There is no end that does not start anew. In every loss, in every grief, there is the hand of comfort, the hand of faith, waiting to move me forward into new ways. I accept the new dominions that come to me through loss. I open my heart to the great and subtle grace that is beginning. All that has gone before, I carry in my heart. My own heart is carried by Life, by love, by the past moving through me, present in me, as it dreams toward the future. I open my heart to the guidance of those I have not lost.

Jump.

JOSEPH CAMPBELL

I HAVE
AN INNER COMPASS

I seek help and guidance in all things. I hear my guidance clearly and respond to it with attention. I am free to choose and free to honor my choices. I act with faith and freedom, moving to express that which is God within me. As I open my life to God's guiding care, my life is transformed.

Develop interest in life as
you see it; in people, things,
literature, music—the world is
so rich, simply throbbing
with rich treasures, beautiful
souls and interesting people.
Forget yourself.

HENRY MILLER

☙

THE UNIVERSE IS IN
CONSTANT CONTACT FOR
MY WELL-BEING

I open my mind and heart to guidance from the Universe. I am open to guidance in all its many forms. I accept help from the Universe through people, events, and places which inspire and instruct me. I listen to the song of Life played through many instruments—through children, animals, the wind, a bird, a flash of sunlight sparkling off glass. All things speak my language. I listen to all languages with my heart. My heart hears higher and higher frequencies of guidance as I raise my own thoughts to the possibility of higher realms guiding and embracing my own.

Trust in yourself. Your perceptions
are often far more accurate than
you are willing to believe.

CLAUDIA BLACK

❦

MY PERCEPTIONS ARE
ACUTE AND ACCURATE

In times of doubt, I remind myself that my sensitivity is acute. I am alert and perceptive. I know—and notice—what I need to know. I register people and events accurately. My antennae are subtle and keen. Denial does not block my perceptions. I am accurate and intuitive. I am shrewd, knowledgeable, sensitive, and clear. Appearances do not deceive me. I sense the truth, respond accurately to reality. I am precisely in tune with my environment. I am grounded and safe. I am sensitive and secure. I am secure because of my sensitivity. It is a divine asset and I use it well.

The real voyage of discovery consists
not in seeking new landscapes,
but in having new eyes.

MARCEL PROUST

❧

MY VISION
IS CLEAR-EYED
AND LONGSIGHTED

I choose reality over denial. I choose clarity over fear. I choose to allow my full potential for clear, grounded thought and action to emerge. I accept divine guidance in its many forms. Guided and clear, I act in my own behalf for my own good and the highest good of others.

The rhythm of my heart is the birth
and death of all that are alive.

THICH NHAT HANH

෯

MY SOUL IS A
COMPASSIONATE HEART

I am compassionate. I allow my heart and imagination to embrace the difficulties and concerns of others. While maintaining my own balance, I find it within myself to extend sympathy, attention, and support. When they are grieved, I listen with openness and gentle strength. I offer loyalty, friendship, and human understanding. Without undermining or enabling, I aid and assist others to find their strength. I allow the healing power of the Universe to flow through me, soothing the hearts and feelings of those I encounter.

I cannot believe that the inscrutable
universe turns on an axis of
suffering; surely the strange beauty
of the world must somewhere
rest on pure joy!

LOUISE BOGAN

☙

MY HEART
IS A VESSEL FOR
TENDERNESS, A BALM
IN DIFFICULTY

I am compassionate toward myself about my own vulnerability. I am tender toward myself in all difficult and challenging times. I accept that I have human limits and human emotions, which I honor and attend to. I allow the Universe to comfort me as I open my eyes and heart to difficult realities.

Learn to get in touch with
the silence within yourself and
know that everything in this life
has a purpose.

ELISABETH KÜBLER-ROSS

⌘

I AM A HEALER
AND MY LOVE
IS MEDICINE

Love is the greatest medicine. I ask to be healing medicine for others. I ask my heart to expand its boundaries and to love others as they wish to be loved. I ask my heart to expand its boundaries and open to my being loved as I wish to be loved.

One day, it was suddenly
revealed to me that everything
is pure spirit.

Ramakrishna

❧

BODY AND SOUL
ARE ONE

There is no separation between body and soul, spirit and matter. One essence, one unity, runs through all of life. This
essence, the God-force, is completely pure, completely perfect. I
claim for myself the health and perfection of this divine force.
My body is beautiful, sacred, and beloved. Spirit infuses my body
with radiant goodness. I experience vitality, enthusiasm, energy,
and power. My physical nature and my spiritual nature are one
and the same. My body's needs and urges are divine in origin. As
I listen to my inner guidance, I move to more and more perfect
health, more and more abundant energy, more and more positive
thoughts, feelings, and actions. My physical body is a conduit for
my spiritual health to pour forth into the world.

Listen. Make a way for
yourself inside yourself.
Stop looking in the other
way of looking.

RUMI

❧

I AM A LISTENER
WITH THE EARS
OF MY SOUL

I listen with the ears of my heart. I am alert to the promptings of love. I respond to the call of love. I answer with faith to move out in love. I listen, am guided, and act upon that guidance with the conviction that good is unfolding through me and to me.

Big-heartedness is the most essential
virtue on the spiritual journey.
MATTHEW FOX

☙

FREEDOM AND DIGNITY CHARACTERIZE MY RELATIONSHIPS

I release all souls from my agendas for them. I surrender my control and my opinions of the growth and right actions of others. I recognize and accept that divine guidance is acting within each of us. I allow others to script their lives and their dealings with me according to their needs and guidance.

We were born to make manifest
the glory of God within us.

NELSON MANDELA

&

CREATIVITY
IS MY BIRTHRIGHT

I am a natural creator. Creativity is the natural order of life. Life is energy—pure creative energy. It is my birthright to co-create my life and my experience. My dreams come from God. The power to fulfill my dreams is God given. There is an indwelling, underlying creative power infusing all of life, including ourselves. When we open ourselves to our creativity, we open ourselves to the Great Creator working with us and within us.

Every child is an artist. The
problem is how to remain an
artist once he grows up.

PABLO PICASSO

❧

MY HEART IS A GARDEN
FOR CREATIVE IDEAS

I recognize that art begins in the heart. I love my creative nature and I love expressing it. I create as an act of love and connection. I allow the Universe to dream through me, to act through me, to create through me.

Why do you weep?
The source is within you . . .

RUMI

❧

MY LIFE IS AT
THE CENTER OF
GOD'S CONSCIOUSNESS

There is no distance in the heart of God. There is no separation. I am in the center of my good. It is unfolding where I am and everywhere. At all times, at all places, I—and everyone—are in the heart of God. There is no leaving God. There is no being left. When I feel most alone, I am still held safely. When I am most afraid, I am still protected. All events, however painful, move toward the good.

I did comprehend the whole world . . .
and the abyss and ocean and all things.
In these things I beheld naught
but divine power.

ANGELA OF FOLIGNO

ALL THAT I CHERISH IS PRECIOUS TO SPIRIT

All that I love is loved by God. Each person that I cherish is in God's heart. There is no beloved whom God cannot aid. There is no difficulty, no barrier which God cannot dissolve. In the heart of all life is the heart of God. Whoever we are, however we pray, our prayers are heard. I pray with confidence for God to act effectively in the lives of those I love. I trust that situations and opportunities will unfold for them in divine order, leading all to the greatest good.

When we create something, we always
create it first in a thought form.

&

I AM EXPERIENCE
EXPANDING

I am born and breathe life into Life. I experience and I expand
experience. Consciously and creatively I realize my full human
potential. It is larger and wider than my individual vision. As I
recognize and commit to my shared humanity, my possibilities
and my abilities increase and multiply. Sourced in God, I am
miraculous. The miraculous is natural.

Any creative endeavor is channeled,
whether it be music or art or
theoretical science. We have the
capacity to tune in to energies
and to convert them into reality
for ourselves.

FRANK ALPER

I AM AN INSTRUMENT OF DIVINE CREATION

I offer myself as a channel for higher creativity. I allow the Universe to work through me. I give over my ideas of limitations and potential. I accept an expanded sense of self. I accept an expanded sense of service. I am guided to grow and I accept that growth freely and without reservation. I allow the pattern of God within me to express its fullest form.

We're afraid of feelings. We
rush through our lives searching
yet not living. For those who
have the interest to look closely,
life becomes art.

Diane Mariechild

 G

TIME IS MY FRIEND

My time is expansive and flexible. I have enough time, more than enough time, to accomplish my dreams and my goals. I use my time wisely. I understand the fluidity of time. I pace myself with ease, claiming my right to determine my own tempo and rhythm, velocity and trajectory through life. Time does not rule me. Time does not dominate me. I work with time as a flexible tool. I relish my use of time.

*Time is the stuff of which
life is made.*

BENJAMIN FRANKLIN

*Without discipline, there's
no life at all.*

KATHARINE HEPBURN

❧

TIME IS MY PARTNER

It is my choice to use time festively and expansively. I have plenty of time, more than enough time. I fill my time with love, expansion, enthusiasm, exuberance, and commitment. I both act and rest at perfect intervals. Proper use of time comes easily to me. I set the rhythm of my days and years, alert to inner and outer cues which keep me in gentle harmony. Time is my friend and my partner. I let it work for me. I breathe out anxiety and breathe in renewal. I neither fight time nor surrender to time. We are allies as I move through life.

❦

MY HEART IS A CHANNEL
FOR DIVINE LOVE

I open my heart to love. I invite the love of the Universe to love through me, nurturing myself and others. I receive and I give love in a natural flow. My love is both steady and ever changing, ever responsive. My love is both constant and flexible. As I give love, I feel love. As I seek to love, I am beloved. I cherish myself as fully and as deeply as I cherish others whom I love.

*When we recognize the Divine
Presence everywhere, then we know
that It responds to us and that
there is a Law of Good, a Law of
Love, forever giving of itself to us.*

ERNEST HOLMES

⁊

MY HEART KNOWS
ITS PARTNER

I open my heart to receiving the love of my true and intended mate. I open my heart to giving love to my true and intended mate. I open to divine guidance regarding our right relationship. I trust completely that I will recognize and be recognized by the soul for whom I am a perfect match. I need no artifice, no ploys, no strategies. My true nature is loving and that is all that is required by this love.

When you see each leaf as a
separate thing, you can see
the tree, you can see the
spirit of the tree, you can
talk to it, and maybe you can
begin to learn something.

WILLIAM J. RAUSCH

☙

MY ENTIRE BEING
IS ALERT AND ALIVE

I accept the guidance which comes to me in subtle forms. I surrender the arrogance of my intellect and embrace its alert intelligence instead. I allow my mind to listen to my heart. I allow my heart to have a voice in my life choices. I embrace both mind and heart, knowing that in partnership they guide me well. There is no circumstance in which I am abandoned. There is no place in which I cannot be found. As I listen to first my heart and then my mind, I find that the Universe does speak to me with gentle clarity. A path does emerge on which I walk with safety.

We believe that the Mind of God
governs all things. We believe that
there is a Divine Intelligence
governing and guiding, counseling
and advising, causing us to
know what to do under every
circumstance and at all times,
if we will but trust it.

ERNEST HOLMES

I AM DIVINELY HELPED,
GUARDED, AND GUIDED

I am always led, always guided. There is no desert, no grief, no wasteland too devastated for the presence of God to find me. I am beloved. I am cherished and seen. I am always heard. Even when my prayers fall on seeming silence, they are heard. God is with me always. I am in God's presence and God is present in me. If I open to guidance, I am always led, always helped. I can hear the voice of God within me. I can hear the urgings of my soul. When I cry out in anguish as being abandoned, even in that despair, the voice of God whispers within me if I will only listen.

All creation is a manifestation
of the delight of God—God seeing
Himself in form, experiencing Himself
in His own actions, and knowing
Himself in us as us.

ERNEST HOLMES

MY TRUE NATURE IS THE
EXPERIENCE OF UNITY

All separation is fear. All fear is illusion. We forget that we are one. We forget that your joy is my joy. Your pain, my pain. In our unity we have communion, compassion, consolation, communication. In our unity, we are one people, one earth, one song. Each of us sings a True Note. Each of us adds to the chorus. Each of us contains the wisdom, the breadth and the height, to encompass all of us in our full humanity. When we remember who we are, we know there is only union, only hope, only good unfolding for us all. When we remember God with us and us within God, fear drops away. Loneliness passes. Reunion and rejoicing fill my heart.

God knows no distance.

CHARLESZETTA WADDLES

☙

NONE ARE LOST AND
ALL ARE FOUND

There is no place or person beyond the reach of God. As I am in God and God is in me and all people, I directly influence people and events through my creative consciousness. Therefore, in a spirit of cooperation and non-coercion, I claim the highest good for all in every circumstance.

❧

MY HEART
IS A THRONE
FOR COURAGE

Life requires courage. All courage that I need is given me by
Life itself. I am guided and supported in every step. I need
only open myself to receiving support and guidance. I honor my
humility in admitting my need for help. I welcome the dignity of
being a fellow among fellows. I honor myself for my courage in
following my guidance.

. . . just a tender sense of
my own inner process, that
holds something of my
connection with the divine.

PERCY BYSSHE SHELLEY

ᝡ

I EXPAND BEYOND
MY FEARS

I relinquish all agendas and timelines originating in my fears. I relinquish all rationalizations and defenses grounded in my fears. I open my heart instead to the healing perspective of compassionate patience for others and myself. I allow myself the luxury of time, the dignity of right action and right timing.

It is life that must be our practice.
It is not enough to hear spiritual
truth or even to have our own
spiritual insights. Every aspect
of what happens to us must become
part of a learning experience.

DIANE MARIECHILD

I AM PARTNERED
BY THE UNIVERSE
IN ALL MY DEALINGS

I lead my life in partnership with the Universe. In all situations I have choices and options which lead me to freedom and expansion. In every time of darkness or difficulty I affirm there is a doorway which will open if I knock. I am never separated from the power of God. There is nothing which stands between me and God. I am within God and God is within me. We are one substance, one energy, one Life.

Over and over, we have to go back
to the beginning. We should not
be ashamed of this. It is good.
It's like drinking water.

NATALIE GOLDBERG

GOD IS ALWAYS WITH ME
AND WITHIN ME

In times of adversity, I accept divine help in my life. I invite, expect, and welcome divine interaction and intervention in my affairs. I recognize there is no circumstance immune to the power of God. I ask and receive divine intervention in my troublesome affairs. I seek and receive direct and active help. I ask for guidance and am assured I receive it. I ask for wisdom, comfort, clarity, and all qualities of which I have need. Because these qualities are within God and God is within me, I always receive my answered prayers.

All substance is energy in motion.
It lives and flows. Money is
symbolically a golden, flowing stream
of concretized vital energy.

THE MAGICAL WORK OF THE SOUL

ॐ

I AM A KINGDOM OF RICH RESOURCES

I am abundantly supplied. As I ask, I receive. As I reach inward, Source flows from me outward. There is no lack, no hesitation. I am directly sourced to universal abundance. My needs are met. My wants are supplied. I draw with confidence upon God-source, knowing that it responds to me with immediate and full attention.

☙

MONEY IS A STRONG
CURRENT FLOWING
TO ME AND THROUGH ME
FOR GOOD

Money is a means to an end. It is a servant and not a master. When I ask for money, I am asking for supply. It may come to me as money, but it may also come to me in other forms. I am alert to the many forms my supply may take. While I welcome and receive money as one form, I also welcome and receive supply in all forms it appears.

Inside you there's an artist you
don't know about. . . .
Say yes quickly, if you know, if you've
known it from before the beginning
of the universe.

RUMI

❧

THE UNIVERSE BRINGS
GIFTS TO MY HEART

I allow the Universe to work through me to give me what it desires. I no longer block my good, my expansion, by greedy demands or by stinginess. Instead, I open my heart and mind to prosperous living. I allow myself to be taught how to live generously and abundantly. God is the gardener and I am the soil. I allow God to fructify my life in all ways.

Explore daily the will of God.

C. G. JUNG

MY TRUST EXPANDS

As I trust, I learn to trust more fully. I honor myself for my bravery in taking risks. As I risk, I learn to risk more fully. Life supports my expansion into a larger and more grounded self. I am able to admit mistakes freely and make course adjustments easily. I see myself as a process, a work in progress. I extend compassion for growing pains to myself and to others.

Our elders used to tell us that
all holy sites are endowed
with ancient wisdom. These
centers have innate powers.

JOSEPH RAEL

ॐ

THE EARTH IS
MY WISE TEACHER

I embrace the wisdom of this earth. I accept my own life's seasonality in all things. I embrace my times of apparent dormancy as well as my showier seasons of growth. I trust the quiet times of apparent absence as the necessary gestation time for a fruitful future.

The aim of life is to live,
and to live means to be aware,
joyously, drunkenly, serenely, divinely aware.

HENRY MILLER

☙

MY FUTURE
BLOSSOMS WITHIN ME

The future is with me now. It is unfolding within me, present and sturdy. My dreams and desires are the seeds of my future. I contain within me everything I need to manifest fully my heart's desires. Since God is within and I am within God, there is no yearning which cannot be satisfied if I will allow its satisfaction. There is no good which cannot come to me if I will allow it to come. It is not necessary for me to "will" the acquisition of some person, event, or situation. I need only align my will to accept the unfolding of my desire.

GOD IS THE GREAT
PHYSICIAN
AND I AM HEALED

I build my physical health upon a spiritual basis. As I turn my attention to the God-force within me, my spiritual health improves, and as it does it strengthens my physical vitality. All sense of strain and exhaustion, all sense of being overwhelmed or fatigued, washes away as I remind myself that God is the source of my energy, the Source of my power. God is the great creator. With God within me, I create radiant good health. I create beauty and serenity within my body. With God within me, I release all negative thoughts and conditions which weaken me physically and spiritually. As I increase my spiritual health, my physical health improves as well. Remembering that my body is a gift from God, I care for it with loving attention and it responds with radiant health.

Today I identify my body with
the action of God, the radiant Life
of the Divine Being. I identify
my physical body with my spiritual
body, claiming they are one and
the same. I know that every aspect
of my body corresponds to the radiant
perfection of the living Spirit.
There is perfection in every part
of my being, perfect wholeness
and completeness.

ERNEST HOLMES

WITH GOD I CREATE FOR MYSELF RADIANT HEALTH

God is the source of my health, the source of my healing. There is no condition that can not be improved through spiritual means. I am in God. God is within me. My prayers are answered both internally and externally. As I remember my own divine nature, as I remember the health and radiance that is God's, I strengthen both my body and my soul. As I open to divine aid, divine support, and a consciousness of divine presence within me, my spiritual and physical health is established. I claim for myself divine help, divine health, divine healing.

Think of yourself as an
incandescent power, illuminated
and perhaps forever talked to
by God and His messengers.

BRENDA UELAND

⁂

I AM A PLANNED AND PRECIOUS CHILD OF SPIRIT

I do not walk alone. I am not friendless. I am led, guided, comforted, and consoled. The earth has plans for me. I am loved and valued. My voice is heard My song is a precious note in the symphony of Life. I remember these things and treat myself with dignity. I am tender toward my fears, compassionate toward my pain. I reassure myself with gentleness that I am not abandoned, never unheard or unseen. I ask Life to meet me with Life. I open my heart and my mind to sign of companionship. I receive friendship in many forms. I recognize love with its many faces. I walk in the companionship of loving guides and guiding love.

To accept the responsibility of
being a child of God is to accept
the best that life has to offer you.
STELLA TERRILL MANN

❧

THE UNIVERSE
CRADLES MY HEART

I find comfort and support from many sources. I am cradled and caressed by loving forces which guide me to my good. I am able, on ever-deepening levels, to feel safe and protected as I move in the world.

Merely looking at the world
around us is immensely different
from seeing it.

FREDERICK FRANCK

I FIND STRENGTH IN
MY KNOWLEDGE

I trust my clarity. I open myself to know what I need to know to see clearly and accurately in all situations. I accept support for my knowledge from all sources. I allow the Universe to hold me in loving arms as I absorb all proper realizations.

Trust that the universe is
working FOR you and WITH you.

SANAYA ROMAN

⁂

MY CHOICES ARE WISE
AND WELL GUIDED

In times of aimlessness, I find focus by seeking the voice of guidance within me. I listen for the promptings of my heart. I am alert to signs and signals in the world around me. I open my thoughts to receive the guidance that may come to me from strangers. Even in times of blindness, I know that I am guided. When I feel I cannot see or hear, even then I am being led. I am not alone. I am not lost. There is no dark grief that cannot be penetrated by the gentle rain of guidance if I will open my heart.

It is only with the heart that one
can see rightly; what is essential
is invisible to the eye.

I LIVE IN
LOVING HARMONY

I draw to me persons who have pure and loving hearts, high ideals, deep compassion, and good humor. I manifest myself a pure, loving, and compassionate heart. I love others through God and God loves others through me. I accept friendships founded in this true love. I offer friendship of this truly loving nature. I encounter love in those I meet and those I meet encounter love in me.

When we pay attention to
nature's music, we find that
everything on the earth
contributes to its harmony.

HAZRAT INAYAT KHAN

ℭ

I DANCE GRACEFULLY TO THE
TIMING OF THE UNIVERSE

I respond gratefully and lovingly to the differing tempos, actions, and needs of others. Recognizing that we partner each other in a great and subtle dance, I accept their growth and their pace as adding to the subtle music of my life. I accept their choices and their actions fully, as guided and dignified as my own. Living in partnership with Life, I accent correction and expansion through the actions of others. I react with love, faith, and dignity when challenged.

Each one of us has all the
wisdom and knowledge we
ever need right within us.
It is available to us through
our intuitive mind, which
is our connection with
universal intelligence.

SHAKTI GAWAIN

❧

I CHERISH MY
INDIVIDUAL INTEGRITY

I honor my own integrity and the integrity of others. I am guided by love. I allow myself to feel the love that is guiding others. Like the earth, I enjoy seasons of renewal. I forgive shortcomings and failures, arrogance and shortsightedness. I allow such human foibles to be dissolved in the graceful flow of life ongoing. Life is a river which flows through me, washing me clean of judgment, cleansing me with the waters of compassion. I allow life to be both tender and clear. I choose the longer view of wisdom over the more short-lived satisfaction of being "right."

If the doors of perception were
cleansed, everything would
appear to man as it is, infinite.

WILLIAM BLAKE

MY HEART IS A VERDANT MEADOW WITH MANY BLOOMS

I open my heart to receiving love and respect. I open my heart to many quarters. I allow my good to come to me from all directions. Remembering that the Universe is my source, I release individuals from any demands that they be the source of my good. I allow the Universe to support me as it chooses, not as I demand. I surrender my narrow vision to a broader and longer view of events. I trust that as I respect and honor myself and others, I will be treated in kind.

I am still learning.

MICHELANGELO

*All of the larger-than-life questions
about our presence here on earth
and what gifts we have to
offer are spiritual questions.
To seek answers to these questions
is to seek a sacred path.*

DR. LAUREN ARTRESS

THE WATERS OF MY SPIRIT
ARE DEEP AND PURE

I draw from the well of universal experience and consciousness. I replenish that well by putting attentive love and kindness into the world. I respect the unity and connection of all things to one another. I live consciously and creatively as part of a sacred unity.

Here in this body are the sacred rivers:
here are the sun and moon as well as
all the pilgrimage places. . . .
I have not encountered another
temple as blissful as my own body.

SARAHA

☙

I AM A BELOVED CREATURE
PRECIOUS TO THE WORLD

I love and I am beloved. I am an integral part of the web of life. I am connected to all things. All things are connected to me. I claim and experience my interconnected divinity. I experience the inner divinity of all things. As I acknowledge and salute the divinity in me and others, I experience harmony and healthy interdependence. All things move through me and with me toward the good.

The meeting of two personalities
is like the contact of two chemical
substances: if there is any reaction,
both are transformed.

C. G. JUNG

&

I DANCE THE DANCE OF LIFE
IN SPIRITED PARTNERSHIP

I discover correction and expansion through the differences I find with others. I react with love, faith, dignity, and curiosity when challenged. I meet each challenge as an opportunity to explore my strengths and my flexibility. I honor my own autonomy and I honor the autonomy of others. I honor my own desires even as I recognize and honor the desires of others. I acknowledge and respect my similarities and my differences with those with whom I interact. I allow my personal universe to be varied and colorful. I grant myself and all I encounter the dignity of our unique individuality and variable needs.

Every time you don't follow your
own inner guidance, you feel a loss
of energy, loss of power, a sense
of spiritual deadness.

Shakti Gawain

MY HEART
HOLDS INTEGRITY

I love integrity. I am authentic in my responses to people and events. I respond with dignity and courage from a core belief that I am worthy. My values are worthwhile. My principles are shaped by my inner knowing, not by my external circumstances. I bring to the changing flow of life events an inner steadiness, an inner compass. I am whole and unified in body, mind, and spirit. My integrity is natural.

No matter how imperfect the
appearance may be, or painful
or discordant, there is still
an underlying perfection, an
inner wholeness, a complete and
perfect Life, which is God.

ERNEST HOLMES

☙

MY PHYSICAL HEALTH
RESTS ON
A SPIRITUAL FOUNDATION

My body is the beloved vessel for my spirit. I treat my body with tenderness and gentle respect. I offer my body friendship and support. My body speaks to me of my spirit's needs. When I need rest, my body asks me to refresh my spirit. When I am hungry, my body asks me to nourish myself, body and soul. When I listen to my body's cues and signals, my spiritual path unfolds with clarity and power. Spirit speaks to me through body. We embody our spiritual lives. As I recognize my body as an equal partner to my spirit, my soul strength increases. As the health of my soul becomes radiant and alive, the health of my body takes on new vitality. Body and soul are one life, one essence. I salute them as loving partners. My body and soul live in vibrant harmony.

All sanity depends on this: that
it should be a delight to feel heat
strike the skin, a delight to stand
upright, knowing the bones are
moving easily under the flesh.

Doris Lessing

THE NATURAL WORLD
IS MY HOME
AND MY HAVEN

I cherish the natural world. I see it in the wisdom of God's un-folding. I surrender my resistance to unfolding fully and beau-tifully. I embrace the mystery of my own evolution. I invite my divine nature to expand and nurture myself and others.

You are a child of God;
your playing small doesn't
serve the world.

NELSON MANDELA

CREATIVITY IS
MY TRUE NATURE

The refusal to be creative is an act of self-will and is counter to our true nature. When we open to our creativity, we are opening to God: good, orderly direction. As we pursue our creative fulfillment, all elements of our life move toward harmony. As we strengthen our creativity, we strengthen our connection to the Creator within. Artists love other artists. Our relationship to God is co-creative, artist to artist. It is God's will for us to live in creative abundance.

God, guard me from those
thoughts
Men think in the mind alone
He that sings a lasting song
Thinks in the marrow-bone.

☙

WE ARE DEEP MUSIC

I am a music waiting to be heard. I am a song unfolding. My notes are the voice of Life singing through me in majesty. I open my throat to the word of creation. I speak my truth and build my life upon it. I open my mouth to exclaim the glory that I feel within me. I give voice to God and God's plan for me. I refuse to be small when God intends for me to be large. I expand without pride, without arrogance. I expand through love. I open my heart and mind to the brighter, clearer, and more joyous vistas Life intends for me. I allow Life to create through me the better life which I speak and see.

cß

I EMBRACE MY
CURRENT REALITY
AND ACKNOWLEDGE
ITS GIFTS

I surrender "if only" agendas for happiness. I find happiness and peace in my current circumstances. I allow goodness to flow to me in every time and in every place. I open to receiving good from any and all sources, at any and all moments. I am alert for my good and I enjoy its many disguised and various forms.

Some people will never learn
anything . . . because they
understand everything too soon.

ALEXANDER POPE

I AM IN RHYTHM
WITH THE FLOW
OF LIFE

I accept divine timing in my life. I surrender control of the tempo of my good's unfolding. I am both eager and patient as my heart is prepared to receive God's gifts of love, friendship, creativity, and abundance. I trust good is coming to pass for me in perfect timing for my highest good.

To be at peace with ourselves,
we need to know ourselves.

CAITLIN MATTHEWS

❧

I
CELEBRATE
MY FULL
HUMANITY

I allow myself to be fully human. I treat myself with loving kindness. I honor and recognize my essential goodness. I honor and recognize my ability to love, to communicate, to share, and to give. I do not have to do any of these things perfectly. There is beauty in the abilities I do have.

Every blade of grass has its Angel
that bends over it and whispers,
"Grow, grow."

MY SPIRIT FINDS
COMPANIONSHIP
IN MANY FORMS

I allow myself to be guided and comforted by the Universe. I allow people and events to gently lead me to my good. I ask for help in all of my affairs and I accept the help that is offered me from many quarters. I do not walk alone. I do not call in vain. Even my whispered dreams are heard by an attentive Universe. I am alert to the help which comes to me for their unfolding.

No more words.
Hear only the voice within.

RUMI

THE UNIVERSE IS MY
GUIDE AND GUARD

The Universe guides and guards its children. I listen and I hear True Guidance, which moves me into loving expansion. I trust my guidance and I act on it faithfully. I move into new territories knowing the way is prepared for me. I walk in safety. My guidance leads me and I follow it with trust.

The will is meant to guide you . . .
so that whatever is appropriate
to any situation is what you
feel like doing and also do.

CEANNE DEROHAN

MY GUIDANCE IS WISE
AND TRUSTWORTHY

I embrace the wisdom of my own inner guidance. I embrace the guidance of my own inner wisdom. I trust, too, the inner wisdom and guidance of others. I trust that others are wise and good.

SANAYA ROMAN

❦

MY HEART IS
A HOME FOR LOVE

My heart is a home for love. I open my heart to compassion, to charity, to respect, and to recognition. I encounter those I meet with openness and with respect. I honor the path that each is walking. I salute in all that I encounter the dignity of God. All differences, all difficulties, are noticed but not condemned. I respect the individuality of every soul. I accept our equality and our brotherhood.

Compassion is the ultimate and most
meaningful embodiment of emotional maturity.
It is through compassion that a person
achieves the highest peak and the deepest reach in
his or her search for self-fulfillment.

ARTHUR JERSILD

THE LOVE IN MY HEART
IS CREATIVE AND
CONSTRUCTIVE

I ask my heart to expand its boundaries and love others as they wish to be loved. I ask my heart to expand its boundaries and open to my being loved as I wish to be loved. I relax my rigid ideas about what love should look like. I open to love's infinite variety. I find love in the face of a flower, love in the glint of sun on a city street. Love walks with me. I carry it in my heart.

Blessings

*Prayers and Declarations
for a Heartful Life*

For those who are our companions

INTRODUCTION

Life is a creative endeavor. It is active, not passive. We are the yeast that leavens our lives into rich, fully baked loaves. When we experience our lives as flat and lackluster, it is our consciousness that is at fault. We hold the inner key that turns our lives from thankless into fruitful. That key is "Blessing."

"My father's house has many mansions," we are told. By counting our blessings, we name ourselves accurately as children of the universe, the richly dowried children of God, or, if you prefer, of "good." Focused on our good, focused on our abundance, we naturally attract more of the same. This is spiritual law. Our consciousness is creative. What we focus on, we empower and enlarge. Good multiplies when focused upon. Negativity multiplies when focused upon. The choice is ours: Which do we want more of?

In every event, in every circumstance, we have a choice of perspective. Faced with difficulty, we can choose between disappointment and curiosity as our mind-set. The choice is ours. Will we focus on what we see as lacking or will we look for the new good that is emerging? In every moment, however perilous or sorrowful it may feel, there is the seed of our greater happiness, greater expansion, and greater abundance.

It is easy to bless events that coincide with our perceived good. When things are going "our way," it is easy to experience faith and gratitude. To bless what might be called "contrary" circumstances requires more faith. Things do not seem to be going our way. In fact, the flow of events may actually run counter to our desires. In all times of such apparent difficulty, it is crucial to bless the flow of events as right and appropriate despite our reservations. The delays, difficulties, and disruptions we experience can in this way enlarge and enrich us. In short, we bless not only the road but the bumps on the road. They are all part of the higher journey.

It is easy, too, to bless people who are sunny and harmonious. It is easy to perceive such personalities as blessings on our path. When people are stormy and temperamental, when people are withholding, mean-spirited, greedy, or judgmental, it is more difficult to bless them, more difficult to perceive their positive contribution to our path. Faced with such unhappy individuals, blessing allows us to lessen their negative impact, to remember that they hold no real power over us. Blessing reminds us that our dignity comes from a divine source. That source is the wellspring of our self-valuing.

The key to practicing blessings is the willingness to accept the full value of each moment. As we are willing to allow each difficult moment to soften and transform into its inner potential, our hearts become hopeful, clear, brave. As we extend the tendrils of our faith above and through the walls of our resistance, our lives become green, verdant, affirming. We are the wild rose basking in the sun. As we cling to our conscious optimism, finding footholds of faith despite opposition, our lives become rooted in the soil of grace. We are nurtured, prospered, and blessed.

The act of blessing is a step into faith. Rather than stand blocked or stymied by circumstances that appear adversarial, we step forward, claiming the safety of our path, the firmness of the soil of God. We affirm, "This is to my benefit. This circumstance blesses my life; I am grateful to this difficult situation for the many gifts it carries. I accept my blessings as they unfold within me."

Counting every blessing is a small step in the direction of our dreams. We gradually perceive our lives on a safe and protected path. Every time we recognize a blessing, it increases our capacity to receive a blessing. As we expand our consciousness in gratitude, we become larger vessels for good. We can consciously and creatively choose to count and encounter our good. We can consciously and creatively choose to expand.

This is easier than it may sound—easier even in the face of very real and very human difficulties.

Blessing a difficulty is not simply accepting it. It is looking at it with new eyes, considering it from a higher, more open-minded perspective. To bless a situation is not to deny its sorrowful or challenging reality. To bless a situation is to claim its inner, hidden reality, a higher, finer working-out of good for all concerned.

To bless a difficult situation, we must soften our hearts to it. When we are in the pain of a difficult realization, we tend instead to wince and steel our hearts against acceptance. We feel the prodding of a pointed awareness and we recoil, fearing it is the point of a lance that will pierce us through.

Blessing is the scalpel of spiritual healing. It removes our poisoned attitudes of fear and constriction, causing the infection of self-importance to flow away, leaving us surrendered and open to the healing action of spirit, the cleansing power of grace. As we surrender resistance, we open our hearts. Freed to love again, they become full, expansive, and wise. We are no longer victimized by resentment and anger. A higher hand is at work.

I take a daily walk with my dogs through a mesa of sagebrush near my house. It was on one of those walks that the idea for this book came to me. It came in the form of what I call my "Marching Orders," what others might call "the still, small voice." One moment I was walking through the sage, breathing in its sweet, heavy scent and enjoying the still-snowcapped mountains that ring Taos valley. The next moment I was "listening" to a startling new direction for my work: I was to write a book of "lessons."

Those lessons would concern an attitude of gratitude, of thankfulness for gifts received.

By now I am used to receiving such creative directives. My walks, in fact, are intended to invite them, but this one surprised me. I already had my writing plans for the next year. Just when did the Guidance think this book would get written and what made it think that I could write it? No sooner had these doubts surfaced than the firm inner voice persisted, "This is what you are to do *now*, next."

I went home and called my editor.

"I know we think we know what I am writing," I began. "But evidently there is something else that I am supposed to do first."

I told my editor the book that had been outlined on my walk.

"So we'll do it," he said.

The book you hold in your hands is that little book. My experience of writing it was one of near anonymity. The prayers and declarations came to me not as things to be written but as things to be written down. I did not so much write this book as transcribe it. I learned from it as I wrote. What I learned is the importance of a practice that Buddhists call "mindfulness," the cherishing of each moment. I prefer the term "heartfulness," as it more closely describes the direction of the lessons that I was given.

May this book yield you a more heartful life.

To bring forth the soul of our being, we must be in our
bodies, rooted to Earth, able to draw from the
universal source of energy.

DIANE MARIECHILD

ॐ

THIS EARTH IS RADIANT
WITH GRACE

The world is abundant. It is filled with beauty. The world holds abundant beauty in people, things, and events. The world offers abundant supply for my every need in people, things, and events. In this generous world, my needs are met through many sources. My desires are fulfilled through many channels. This world is sacred, bountiful, and generous. I recognize and appreciate this abundance. I have the courage to desire my good and I have the expectations of my good being fulfilled. I am partnered and provided for by universal flow. I am enriched by universal supply. Carefully and consciously, I am cared for in earthly ways by divine sources. My good is assured. I prosper in this abundant world.

God, I can push the grass apart
And lay my finger on Thy heart.

EDNA ST. VINCENT MILLAY

CⱲ

A BROAD AND RADIANT
RIVER OF GOODNESS FLOWS
SURELY THROUGH MY LIFE

Divine flow prospers my endeavors. Divine supply funds my dreams. I open my heart to divine action in all my affairs. I am ready and able to act on divine guidance as it unfolds within me and outside of me in every circumstance. When I am lonely and overwhelmed, I remind myself I am partnered by a loving universe. I turn my attention inward, seeking a state of calm. I listen both within and without for promptings—signs, signals, and communications—that ease my soul and allow it to act wisely and decisively.

For several centuries now, we have overemphasized the
intellect. It is fine in its place. It is not, however,
the most authentic way of knowing. The most
authentic comes from the heart.

SONIA CHOQUETTE

MY HEART IS A WISE
AND FAITHFUL GUIDE

I bless the wisdom of my loving heart. Love is a form of listening. I listen with a loving heart. I listen to the love within my heart and I hear the love in the hearts of others. My heart guides me tenderly and truly. I find ways through the wilderness. My heart finds paths through the desert. My heart is valiant and wise. My heart senses the truth and offers compassion in times of conflict. My heart has patience. My heart has humility. It is fully human and fully divine. As I listen to my heart, I am able to love humanly with divine wisdom. I am wiser than I know, kinder than I believe. I am loving and compassionate to others and myself. My heart holds the world in tender awe.

All you need to do to receive guidance is
to ask for it and then listen.

SANAYA ROMAN

I TRUST MY INNER WISDOM

I consciously validate my perceptions. I count myself as a valuable, insightful, and objective observer of life. Looking at my life and my situation, I applaud my capacity for wise choices, discerning actions. I am more clear-eyed and perceptive than I have often thought. At this time I consciously recall situations in which my own clarity and sense of the unfolding of events were borne out to be true and accurate. Rather than focus on the times when I have made mistakes or suffered errors of judgment, I focus instead on the many times when I have seen clearly, acted properly, and been rewarded for my wisdom by a happy unfolding of events. My acuity is a great blessing for me and others.

The light which shines in the eye is really the light of the heart. The light which fills the heart is the light of God.

Rumi

⁓

MY WORLD IS A WORLD
OF LOVE AND MY LOVE IS
A LOVING WORLD

My heart is a home for God. God is a home for my heart. I am large enough to hold God's entire world within me. I am small enough that God's entire world holds me also in its heart. There is no separation between hearts. There is no distance. Love is the substance of all life. Everything is connected in love, absolutely everything. When I focus my heart on the love of a person, I am connected to that person. As I open to compassion and freedom for others, I find compassion and freedom for myself. We are all loved. We are all loving. We are all love seeking to express itself in love and in so doing receive love in return. When I listen to love, I am listening to my true nature. When I express love, I am expressing my true nature. All of us love. All of us do it more and more perfectly. The past has brought us both ashes and diamonds. In the present we find the flowers of what we've been and the seeds of what we are becoming. I plant the seeds of love in my heart. I plant the seeds of love in the hearts of others. We are God's garden, as God is our own. Our garden grows more beautiful as we recognize and realize who we are. We are love becoming more loving, becoming more loved as we know who we are. I love the world and those I share it with. The world I share shares love.

*You must remember that man is noble, man is sublime, man
is divine, and can accomplish whatever he desires.*

SWAMI MUKTANANDA

☙

I OPEN MY HEART TO LOVE
WITH AN OPEN HAND

My gift for unconditional love is a great blessing in my life. I am able to manifest an inner nobility in my relationships. I accept those who love me as they are. I allow them to love me at their speed and tempo as they are able. I do not dictate or control. Their love for me is a gift. I allow them the right to choose how and when they can give it. Those who love me are part of God's love for me. They are a part of the larger plan of my life. I allow God to remain the whole. I root myself in God, accepting the relationships which come to me as a part of something larger that holds all of us within its scope. I find the steadiness of divine companionship. I allow God to be my primary security, the deep soil of my heart's safety. Rooted in God, I allow human love to gift me and grace me but I do not demand a godlike security from human love. I find perfect love, perfect security, and perfect safety in God. I allow my human loves to be human and I love them in their humanity.

I am at peace with the community of life.

LOUSIE L. HAY

ॐ

MY FRIENDSHIPS ARE
GROUNDED IN GOD

My love is sourced by divine love, shaped by divine guidance, prospered by divine power. I cherish my friendships. Rooted in God, they are flexible and enduring. They are honest, heartfelt, and healthy. I maintain deep affections without fear of abandonment. Knowing all souls are part of God and God is part of all souls, I see my friends as divine in nature and origin while human in form. Recognizing our divine origins, I am serene and secure in the underlying communion of grace in which we dwell.

All life is vibration. You combine with what you notice, or you combine with what you vibrate to. If you are vibrating to injustice and resentment you will meet it on your pathway, at every step.

FLORENCE SCOVEL SHINN

ॐ

I AM OPENHEARTED
AND EXPANSIVE

I am blessed with a hospitable heart. I welcome new souls into my family of souls. I open my heart to new companions. I am a field warm with the sun. My grasses wave green and abundant. As I welcome new life, my heart blossoms with new flowering. New friendships, new experiences, new thoughts, ideals, and insights come to me as I practice openhearted acceptance of life's abundant gifts. As my life expands in volume and velocity, I remind myself that God is the ground of my being. All people and events are rooted in divine consciousness. All unfold together for my greater good. Even as I welcome the new, I salute and release the old. I allow people and events to pass from my sphere, wishing them well, wishing them love and fulfillment on their journey. All that I have loved, I do love. My heart expands to allow greater and greater freedom to those whom it loves. My heart blesses its beloveds with the double gift of freedom and connection.

℘

MY FREEDOM IS THE
GATEWAY TO A LARGER LIFE

I cherish my freedom to act, think, feel, and choose as I wish. I celebrate the choice which lies for me in every moment. I accept the responsibility which comes with freedom. I embrace my liberty and use it to create an abundant and meaningful life. I gratefully acknowledge the expansive opportunities my freedom allows me. I recognize that the shape of my life can largely be of my own choosing. Knowing that I am free, accepting that I am free, relishing that freedom and using it to build a life built upon my true values, I am fortunate and know that that is so.

☙

I CO-CREATE MY LIFE
THROUGH CONSCIOUS
CHOICE

Life is intentional, not accidental. I bless this central fact. Consciousness instigates shifts in outer reality. Recognizing that I have the power to change my world by changing my thinking, I set for myself a gentle vigilance toward negative thoughts. When I fear abandonment, I remind myself that the universe itself is my loving companion. When I fear stagnation, I surrender into the deeper flow of life rather than willfully forcing artificial solutions. Constantly partnered by an interactive universe, I do my part by reminding myself that I am part of a larger plan, partnered by an infinite intelligence. In its perfect pink blossoming, the bloom of the apple tree does not concern itself with whether a bee will appear. The blossom does its job just by blossoming. The bee is drawn to do the rest. Rather than imagine that my yearnings are self-centered or counter to the flow of life, I practice simply blossoming in the faith that I attract what I need simply by following and blessing my true nature.

There is a vitality, a life force, an energy, a quickening, that is translated through you into action, and because there is only one of you in all time, this expression is unique. And if you block it, it will never exist through any other medium and will be lost.

ତ

THE BREATH OF SPIRIT
BREATHES THROUGH ME

I am a unique conduit for the good of the universe to flow into the world. As I listen and respond to my inner guidance, I bring to the world originality and opportunity. I have a unique healing presence which blesses those who know me. As I open my heart to being true to my own nature, I provide for others a personal and providential medicine. We do not interact by mistake. I am placed where I am and with whom I am for many important reasons. As I become more fully myself, my individual personality brings specific gifts to those who surround me. As I open myself to unfolding my own inner gifts, the gifts of my nature grace others in outward and material ways. My presence in this world is important. My attitudes and actions have importance. As I choose to be a healing and creative presence, I am a balm for a troubled world. The grace of Spirit touches me and through me touches all I encounter.

It is right and necessary that we should be individuals.

The Divine Spirit never made any two things alike—

no two rosebushes, two snowflakes, two grains

of sand, or two persons. We are all just a little unique

for each wears a different face; but behind each

is the One Presence—God.

ERNEST HOLMES

❧

WE ARE PRECIOUS JEWELS
IN THE CROWN OF SPIRIT

Each of us is unique, valuable, worthy, and irreplaceable. Each of us is kind, wise, knowing, and gifted. Each of us is filled with dignity, gifted with humor, funded with strength. We are met as equals. We bear gifts for each other. Our hearts are true friends, true colleagues. We have a place with each other. We have a need for each other. All of us seek the same answers, although we find them by different routes. All of us hold the same questions although we express them in different ways. Our loving hearts hold the solutions all of us seek. This is a great blessing and indisputable fact. In loving each other, we love the world. In loving each other, we find the world. The world we find is healed by our loving hearts.

The world of reality has its limits;
the world of imagination is boundless.

JEAN-JACQUES ROUSSEAU

❧

MY SOUL INHABITS MANY
WORLDS WITH COMFORT

Distance and diversity are part of me. I bless my width and depth. All that is foreign and unfamiliar is yet a part of who I am. Mine is the family of man. My tribe inhabits the earth, walking in different lands, speaking in different tongues but living one life as we go forward. Knowing that I am a part of all life, I cherish differences. I embrace diversity. Recognizing that all faces and forms are my own face and form, I treat myself and others with dignity. We are brothers. We are sisters. We are husband and wife, mother and father. We are a family of many colors and many cloaks. We are one life. The language of the heart speaks to us all. I cherish that which my brother cherishes. I walk in harmony, generosity, and abundance. I share my gifts from the gifts I share.

If you look deeply into the palm of your hand, you will see
your parents and all generations of your ancestors. All of
them are alive in this moment. Each is present in your body.
You are the continuation of each of these people.

THICH NHAT HANH

⁂

THE BLOOD OF LIFE
FLOWS THROUGH ME

We are not alone. We are privileged to carry in our blood and bone the wisdom of those who have gone before us. We carry their lives, even in the face of their deaths. In each of us there survive the lives of those who gave us life. In our children, and in our brainchildren, our own lives go forward. Faced with the loss of a human love, I turn to the divine love within me which can accept that loss, embrace that loss, and carry forward the beloved whom I feel to be beyond reach. God is in me and I am in God. All that ever was, still is. We are a divine energy, a divine life. In our dying, we live again. In our living, we die again.

There is no loss which is not a gain carried forward. In my moments of greatest sorrow, I am touched by the joy of having loved. In my times of greatest loss, I am still loved. Love is not lost through loss. It is found more fully. I cherish the love my loss has helped me find.

People talk about nature. As the water moves, it makes its
own sound. As the wind blows, it makes its own sound.
When fire burns, it makes its own sound. In the same
way, all of us have that music going on.

Swami Chidvilasananda

⌘

THE MELODY OF LIFE
FLOWS THROUGH ME

The song of life is infinite and variable. Its melodies and harmonies hold infinite possibilities. I am both the listener and the song. I am both the composer and the note. A creator myself, I am also the creation of a larger hand. In the great symphony of life, I am both large and small. I welcome this paradox. I allow myself to feel the protective guidance of a greater whole even as I allow myself to feel the power of my own largeness and strength. The balance is perfect, the design sublime. Recognizing that I am small enough to receive help and large enough to give it, I both receive energy and extend energy with a rhythm as melodic and as natural as breathing. Conscious of this process, I know that I can inhale greater support when that is my need, and exhale greater support when that is the need of others. My life is lived in harmony. I am a graceful note consciously and organically connected to the universal song. As I am true to myself, those who are in harmony with me resonate to my personality and come to my side. Knowing that, I count myself blessed. I find myself both powerful and protected.

We must be aware of the real problems of the world.
Then, with mindfulness, we will know
what to do and what not to do
to be of help.

THICH NHAT HANH

❧

WE ARE TRUSTWORTHY
STEWARDS OF OUR WORLD

The world is a work in progress. We are the architects of a better world. In our hearts, we hold compassion, invention, clarity, and hope. We know right action. We know wisdom. We know divine intent. The world is safe in our keeping. We are loving. We are wise. We are good. We can change our world for the better. We can bring our best to the world. The whole world lies within each of us. Our every thought and act touch all. I am powerful. We are powerful. As I make my inner world gentle, harmonious, and joyful, I bring those qualities to the world which all of us share. I cherish the world which we share. I bless the world and those I share it with.

Loneliness is the way by which destiny
endeavors to lead man to himself.

HERMANN HESSE

☙

I AM A VESSEL
FOR DIVINE ENERGY

My heart is a chalice for love. I am well loved. I open my heart to feel that I am loved. I allow myself to be saturated by love. I soften my heart and gently ask it to receive the love I encounter. I do not need to earn love. I do not need to work at love. I need only to allow myself to feel the love extended toward me. I need only to accept love to know that I am lovable. I choose to remember—and cherish—the ways in which I am loved.

For Mercy has a human heart,
Pity a human face,
And Love, the human form divine.

WILLIAM BLAKE

☙

I LOVE OTHERS
FOR THEIR
TRUE SELVES

I bless and salute the divine goodness available for all human beings and in all human beings. I allow people to be uniquely
themselves, bringing their true natures and true gifts to our relationships. I do not demand that those who love me change their
essential nature for my comfort. I express to them my nature. I tell
them my truth. I do not hide or pretend I am different from what
I am. I trust that each of us is a perfect part of the divine whole.
I trust that each of us is as lovable as we are. I allow originality, in-
ventiveness, and variability in my loving relationships. I invite the
unique souls in my life to love me as their true selves allow.

☙

I AM A FOUNTAIN
IN THE LIGHT

As I bless all I encounter, all I encounter blesses me. Joy and well-being pour forth from my contented heart. I am sourced by divine power. A divine force flows out from me into the world. All I encounter are touched by the divine spark within me. I am touched by the divine spark within all others. Meeting a stranger, I see the familiar face of God. Meeting adversity, I see the hidden face of God. There is no situation so foreign that I do not claim and recognize good working through it and in it. When I encounter sorrow, I open my heart to contain and transform it. I allow the action of loving compassion to alchemize all difficulty into an opportunity to find the hidden face of God and cherish it.

At the height of laughter, the universe is flung into
a kaleidoscope of new possibilities.

JEAN HOUSTON

I ANTICIPATE GREAT GOOD
AND OPEN MY HEART TO IT

I am alert to new beginnings. I open my heart to bless the "hello" that comes to me uninvited and unexpected. I bring to my world a child's openness to new companions. I allow myself to be met. In the face of new beginnings, I practice curiosity and expansion. I embrace risk and I open to play. Mine is a festive heart. I do not allow old songs and old ideas to become the only melodies I will listen to. I practice a listening heart. I am attentive to the pipings of small adventures. Even in the face of haste, even in the light of past experience, I entertain optimism, allow enthusiasm, encourage care. My heart is resilient and expansive. I cherish all that I have and welcome my ability to care still further for all that yet is offered me.

Humor is not a mood but a way of looking at the world.

LUDWIG WITTGENSTEIN

The situation is critical . . . but not serious.

SONIA CHOQUETTE

☙

MY HUMOR LIGHTS
THE WORLD

I am blessed by wit and humor. I see the light side of dark times. I see the antic grace in awkwardness, the comic foibles in human nature. I am serious in my commitments but I am lighthearted in my fulfillment of them. I allow myself to feel the support of universal forces. This connection to spiritual reality allows me to move more lightly through the world. My laughter is a great bell blessing my life. My friendships are graced by humor and shared laughter. My spirituality is grounded in joy. Humor blesses my world.

Enthusiasm means "of the gods." When you have an
enthusiastic heart, all the heavens can flow through it.

SONIA CHOQUETTE

&

MY ENTHUSIASM FUNDS ME
WITH POWER

I am blessed by the gift of an enthusiastic heart. I respond to life with lively interest, with contagious joy, with ardor and delight. My enthusiasm is a spiritual wellspring. It graces me with energy. It fills me with passion and with the perseverance to see that passion out. My enthusiasm is a fuel for my endeavors. It is a fire which warms me and my friends. I greet the world with a lover's open heart. I do not allow cynicism or skepticism to sour my attitudes.

☙

MY SENSE OF TOUCH GIFTS
ME WITH PLEASURE

I take pleasure in my sense of touch. It grounds me in the physical world. It connects me to my surroundings. The silken feel of a baby's hair, the sleek coat of a dog, the satiny feel of my lover's skin, the sleek hide of a horse—all these bring me pleasure. The cool blessing of water, the hot gift of soup, the warmth of the sun, the gentle touch of wind—all these grace me with their feel.

My sense of touch receives love and expresses it. My sense of love receives care and expresses it. My sense of touch allows my soul to meet the world intimately, sweetly, and with ardor. I bless my sense of touch and savor all that it brings to me.

The sky is the daily bread of the eyes.

RALPH WALDO EMERSON

☙

MY SENSE OF SIGHT
CONNECTS ME TO MY WORLD

The exquisite line of a lover's hand, the graceful shape of an apple-laden bough dipping in the wind, the contour of a mountain's flank, the cottony fluff of a dandelion gone to seed—my eyes cherish these sights and many more. My child's first steps, my father's ailing walk, the dance of flowers windblown in a meadow—my eyes witness all of these.

I cherish the sights I behold. I savor the sights I see. My gift of sight brings me the gift of insight. I bless the vision brought to me by vision.

We are all, in a sense, music.

Don Campbell

❧

I AM A FLUTE FOR THE MUSIC OF GOD'S LOVE

I am a conduit for divine kindness to pour forth into the world. As I make of my heart a loving balm for those in difficulty, I find I, too, am soothed, for compassion pours out from me as a grace which heals me and heals others. There is no wound which does not benefit from human kindness. Compassion is divine in nature but human in expression. As I resolve to be a gateway for kindness to enter the world, I am led myself into a kinder world. As I extend myself in generosity and warmth, my world becomes warmer and more generous. The vessel of my heart is sourced in God. Drawing on this divine source, my supplies of love are boundless. Remembering that divine love loves through me, I am able to love freely and without exhaustion. Drawing on universal love, I am able to cherish others and myself.

We are part of the vast continuum of existence that
includes all things conscious, unconscious, inert, physical,
mental, emotional, known and unknown, imaginable
and unimaginable.

SUSAN BAKER

ᑯ

THE SEASONS OF MY HEART
HAVE PURPOSE AND
MEANING

I bless my connection to all that is. In times of doubt and despair, I turn my attention to the natural world. Recognizing that all things have seasons of growth and birth, seasons of decay and gestation, I allow myself to experience the cyclicality in my own life. Where I experience loss, I anticipate future growth. Where I experience emptiness, I anticipate an inflow of the new. Where I experience doubt and dismay, I welcome a resurgence of faith and conviction. I allow my life to be tidal. I allow my life to fill and empty according to a plan higher than I might naturally perceive. Out of my periods of drought and desolation, I affirm that new growth occurs, funded in deeper strength due to my times of testing and difficulty. It is all for the good, I remind myself. There is a purpose and a point to all I undergo. My pain engenders in me a compassionate heart toward the pain of others. When I suffer, I remind myself that my suffering carries a gift within its hardship, a goal within its trial. Choosing to recognize the powerful good within my adversity, I bless all seasons of my life for their wealth and value.

❦

MY CREATIVITY FUNDS
THE CREATIVITY OF ALL

My creativity is an act of my soul. I am rooted in the creativity of the entire universe. My dreams and desires are funded by divine power, intended to bring divine good and harmony into the world. As I lovingly act in the direction of my dreams, I help manifest the dreams and desires of those whom I meet along the way. My dreams prosper and encourage the dreams of others. There is no competition, no devaluing of others to reach my goals. As I flower creatively, I give to others the gift of my example. As I become larger and more magnificent, I am a show of the power of Spirit to make all of us fuller and more abundant. There is in me only goodness, only grace. My creative dreams are blessings for the world. As I bless others through my art and artfulness, others are encouraged to flower in return. We are a garden growing into glory. I am a bloom whose glory brings beauty to all. My dreams are important to the unfolding of the world.

⁂

THIS WORLD IS MAGICAL
IN ITS DIVERSITY, ABUNDANT
IN ITS BLESSINGS

My abundance comes to me in many forms. My life is abundant in multiple ways. I savor its specific abundance. I cherish its particular multiplicity. Loving humor, a tender smile, a compassionate conversation—all of these are forms of my abundance. Beauty in nature, the bounty of good food, music, the delight of sunlight on the skin—this is my abundance. The scent of flowers, the smell of newly mown grass—this is my abundance. The smile of a stranger, the leap of a cat, the sound of bells—this is my abundance. The satisfaction of a job well done, the pay for services rendered, the thank-you of gratitude—this, too, is my abundance. I recognize and enumerate life's generous gifts and hold them as blessings in my heart.

You are the comfort of my soul in the season of sorrow.
You are the wealth of my spirit in the heartbreak of loss.

RUMI

❧

I AM HELD IN
COMPASSIONATE ARMS

The universe is tender toward my heart. I count this a great blessing and I trust it. Frightened, threatened, or overwhelmed, I place my emotional safety in the hands of a loving universe. I ask for protection, wisdom, and discernment. Knowing that I am cared for and protected, I am alert for support and security coming to me from many directions. I find supportive people, comforting events, unexpected and gracious encounters. The world is not a hostile place. I am aided and safe. The world is my home. I am aided, safe, and protected.

True life is lived when tiny changes occur.

LEO TOLSTOY

❧

I AM ALERT
TO MY BLESSINGS

I open my eyes, ears, and heart to the goodness all around me. Rather than focus on grandiose moments of dramatic change, I focus instead on the slight, steady, constant flow of improvement in my life. In every circumstance, in each encounter, I tabulate a small, hidden blessing. I allow God to guide me into new eyes, clearer vision, the insight necessary to count and encounter my abundance. My desire to see my abundant blessings gives me eyes to see. My desire to hear my blessings gives me ears to hear. The desire of my heart to encounter and explore my blessings opens my inner horizons to depths and heights which are expansive, inspiring, and beautiful. I bless the alert attention which connects me to this world.

The present moment is filled with joy and happiness.

If you are attentive, you will see it.

THICH NHAT HANH

☙

BLESSINGS BUILD
UPON BLESSINGS

I choose to see and build upon the good of every moment. In counting my blessings, I consciously and concretely build a life of gratitude. A life of gratitude is a life built upon optimism, expectation, and attention to the good of every instant as it unfolds. This is not denial of adversity. Rather, the choice to consciously count—and encounter—my moment-to-moment good is a spiritual discipline. My trained optimism creates in me a stamina funded in the constant flow of minute but perceptible spiritual nutrients which fuel me, body and soul. I bless my conscious attention to good.

My crippled poetry began to dance
with the light of God's Name.
His Name brought the angel of words
into the house of my mind.

ॐ

THE GREAT CREATOR
CREATES THROUGH ME

My heart is a wellspring of creative ideas. I acknowledge the blessing of my abundant inner life. Sourced—and resourced—by spirit, I am a Source of healing and inspiration for myself and others. As I reach within me in a spirit of exploration and expansion, I feel my inner horizon enlarge as I recognize larger and better possibilities for myself and for the world. When I turn to myself and my inner promptings with kind attention, I find I have many ideas and inspirations about what I can do to improve the quality of life for myself and for others. I turn with delight and anticipation to my own Inner Voice. I lis-

ten with care to its whispered suggestions. I act on the Guidance
I receive and my actions, concrete and well intentioned, alter the
quality of the life I lead and the life that others lead with me. My
inner life blesses my outer world.

Listen to your own Self.
If you listen to that Self within, then you find the Truth.

KABIR

I ACCEPT MY BLESSINGS AS
THEY UNFOLD WITHIN ME

I am blossoming in Spirit's time. Knowing this, I turn to my inner flowering securely. Within the environment of my own heart, I enjoy the sunlight of safety, the warmth of harmony, the strength of right companions. Focused on the reality that Spirit is my constant companion, I remember to be comforted by the continuity of my blessings. Grounded in the safety of divine presence, I am able to breathe deeply, pause in my striving, and notice the unfolding of one gift into another. My life is evolutionary and revolutionary. My attitude of openness, expectation, and observation yields me a sense of abundance.

Love is not a possession. It is the flow of God's energy.

Swami Chidvilasananda

☙

FAITH MOVES ME
TO RIGHT ACTION

I see life as a series of choices. This recognition blesses me with active faith. I choose to make my choices positive and life affirming. In the face of depression and a sense of despair, I find a small action which I can undertake toward the positive. Recognizing that my life is a matter both of proportion and perception, I work consciously to keep gratitude as my chosen attitude and optimism as the lens through which I view the world. This is not denial. This is courage. Rather than surrender to feelings of negativity and despair, I consciously and creatively combat such feelings by moving in the direction of greater faith. Rather than rehearse catastrophe, I use my thinking to remember the ever-present potential for happiness and health. I take my cue from the resilience of life itself.

The wren is small but active in the face of threatening odds. So too I choose to take personal and positive actions in the face of planetary negativity. Rather than wallow in hopelessness, I enact the viability of hope. I reach out to others with kindness and humor. I allow others to reach toward me bearing their gifts of love and healing. Rather than isolate, I communicate. I signal the world that I am engaged, committed, and active for the greater good. My active faith blesses all.

The infinite richness of the Father is mine to enjoy. The vital

good health, the wisdom, the peace, and all the good things

which proceed from the Father I now claim. The act

of accepting them is my right and privilege and I

exercise it intelligently and in full faith.

Life now sings through me in radiant ecstasy.

ERNEST HOLMES

I AM A CHILD OF
DIVINE ABUNDANCE

It is my father's pleasure to give me the kingdom." By opening our hearts to receive from the universe, we achieve our proper position in relation to spiritual law. Spirit intends to flow to us and through us. We are intended to allow this flow. Focusing on the tiny increments of good which come to us daily, we count our blessings. Counting every blessing as a small step in the direction of my dreams, I gradually perceive my life as a safe and protected path leading in the direction of my dreams. Every time we recognize a blessing, we increase our capacity to receive a blessing. As we expand our consciousness in gratitude, we become larger vessels for good. I consciously and creatively choose to count and encounter my good. I consciously and creatively choose to expand.

Show love to all creatures and you will be happy;

for when you love all things, you love the Lord,

for He is all in all.

TULSIDAS

❧

I AM A TRUE NOTE IN THE SYMPHONY OF LIFE

The pace of the universe brings harmony to my soul. My heart opens to the divine timing which best serves my soul. My heart paces itself according to divine unfolding. I accept and appreciate the pacing of my life. I recognize that as I seek to align myself with higher wisdom, my path is led perfectly, a step at a time, for my own highest unfolding. Spirit is the Great Conductor. I am given my cues. There is no need for haste. There is no place in me for impatience. Delays and detours to my limited vision are actually the perfect path unfolding to a higher eye. Knowing that divine timing is perfect and that I am a divinely loved child of the universe, I surrender my anxiety and urgency. I allow higher forces to orchestrate the good which is mine to have.

There is a place where words are born of silence,
A place where the whispers of the heart arise.

RUMI

❧

I AM DIVINELY PARTNERED
AND LED

I am blessed by the guidance of Spirit in many forms. I open my heart and my mind to the influence of higher forces. I relinquish my definition of myself as small and limited. I invite guidance and inspiration. I welcome new thoughts and perceptions, larger perspectives and possibilities. Rather than insist on being the sole author of my life, I invite the collaborative forces of the universe. Synchronicity, coincidence, reinforcement, and serendipity—these are friendly companions which speak to me clearly of higher realms. Rather than close my mind to the possibility of active spiritual intervention in my affairs, I commit to noticing, noting, and acknowledging the support which I actually receive. Life is an orchestra. I am at once a musician, a music, a conductor, a composer, and an audience. I recognize my multiple roles and I embrace the harmonics of my accompaniment. I am perfectly, intricately partnered. I count this partnership a central blessing in my life.

Stand up and play the melody,
I am God.

◈

MY HEART KNOWS
ITS TRUE NAME

Divinity is my true nature. I am a soul among souls. I intersect those people whom I am meant to meet. Our paths cross by divine providence, not by chance or misdirection. We are blessed in our connection. Knowing this, I encounter all I meet with curiosity and gracious hospitality. I open my heart to receive them and I open my mind to acknowledge the insights and information which they bear. In every encounter, I respond and react from a position of curiosity and kinship. My heart is not closed. My heart is not defended. I am an equal among equals, a learner among learners, a friend among friends. As I seek, I too am sought. I am drawn to the people who best companion me. The people I best companion are drawn to me. My heart is secure in its divine origin. Resting in that security, I meet all souls with the recognition of their godhood, their divine spark, their dignity. Extending myself in compassion and companionship, I journey through the world with a tender and a welcoming heart. I bless this world and it blesses me in return.

When we are really honest with ourselves we must admit
our lives are all that really belong to us. So it is how we use
our lives that determines the kind of men we are.

CESAR CHAVEZ

ॐ

THE WORLD IS BOUNTIFUL ENOUGH FOR ALL ITS CHILDREN

The world is abundant. There is enough for all of us. This is the great truth and blessing. I do not need to hoard. I do not need to grab for more. My good coexists with the good of others. What is best for me and what is best for all are one and the same. I open my heart to the highest outcome. I open my heart to the universal good. My blessings come to me freely. I do not need to compete for them. My blessings bless others as well. There is abundance for all, a right place for all. I open my heart to divine guidance in finding my right place.

To work with God-power you must give it right-of-way
and still the reasoning mind. The instant you ask,
Infinite Intelligence knows the way of fulfillment. Man's part
is to rejoice and give thanks, and act his Faith.

FLORENCE SCOVEL SHINN

☙

THE WORLD BEFRIENDS ME

The world befriends me. In times of pain and loneliness, I ask God to open my eyes to the companionship found in the natural world. I ask to see beauty, feel grace, and know that I am partnered at all times, in all ways, by the million hands the universe sends to guide and accompany me on my travels. While I may long for contact with one special person, I ask to see the specialness in all whom I meet. I ask to be a light and a comfort to those whom I encounter. Even when troubled by loneliness, I take time to extend myself to others. Blessing the world which befriends me, I befriend the world.

In necessary things, unity; in disputed things, liberty;
in all things, charity.

☙

CHARITY GRACES MY VIEW
OF THE WORLD

Mine is a charitable heart. It is rooted in the wisdom of compassion. It is fed by the springs of self-love. Taking a compassionate view of myself and others, I act in the world with gentle temperance. I am not rash in action, harsh in judgment, quick in condemnation of those I see. My heart is a peaceable kingdom. Love rules its territory. Love shapes its laws.

I bless my personal charity and I choose it. My charity is born not of denial but of respect. I consciously choose to view all beings as having both dignity in their current selves and the potential to be ever more beautiful as they expand those selves. This being the case, when people grieve or disappoint me, I remind myself that the seeds of future greatness still lie within them and that my forgiving grace may be exactly the support which they need.

My charity makes me a willing servant but not a doormat. As kind as I am to others, I practice being kinder still to myself. Remembering that each of us carries the flame of divinity, I bless that flame in myself, husband its light, and then extend its charitable glow to others.

It is within my power either to serve God or not to serve him.
Serving him, I add to my own good and the good of the whole
world. Not serving him, I forfeit my own good and deprive
the world of that good, which was in my power to create.

LEO TOLSTOY

☙

SERVING THE WHOLE,
I FEEL MYSELF TO BE
A CHERISHED PART

In every moment, I am given opportunities for creative service. Sometimes that service is simple witness: I count and encounter the blessings of life. I recognize and honor the dignity of those whom I meet. Other times, the service is more heartfelt: I reach within myself to console and comfort those who are suffering and in need. There is one substance flowing through all. That substance is love. As I choose to align myself in service to its nature and my own, I also serve by example. This service is not thankless martyrdom. Loving service is an act of enlightened self-love. As I focus on others, my own troubles and losses fall into perspective. Acknowledging the worth of those I encounter, I recognize my own worth. Seeking to serve, I serve myself by experiencing the truth of my loving and expansive nature. This self-knowledge is a great blessing.

Do not weep; do not wax indignant. Understand.

ॐ

KINDNESS IS MY NATURE
AND MY GIFT

My heart is a deep lake of loving-kindness. I count myself fortunate to hold tenderness within my soul. I forgive myself my fears, frailties, and failures. I am compassionate toward myself in times of turbulence and change. I remind myself that I am a gentle soul and that I have need of cherishing. I treat myself as I wish others would treat me. I treat others as they wish to be treated. I allow myself, in times of difficult and demanding strife, that I am loved and lovable, that I am worthy and respected. I do not allow temporary anxiety to distort my view of the whole. I gently seek the blessings in all difficulty while I am compassionate to myself for my lingering doubts and fears. I remind myself that my life is in the care of God and that it is unfolding with beauty and harmony.

I saw my Lord with the eye of my heart, and I said:
Who art Thou? He said: Thou.

AL-HALLAJ

&

I KNOW MY TRUE NAME

I am a divine child and I delight in my companionship. I love myself. I enjoy my own company. I take delight in my interests, my diversions, my pastimes. I approve of myself. I honor my choices. I seek and I find integrity within my soul. I am comforted by my own companionship. I am a friend to myself. I encounter my thoughts and emotions tenderly and with interest. I have patience with myself. I do not expect too much. I am not harsh or critical. With warm support and affection I encourage my own unfolding. I trust myself to have intimacy with my own needs, wants, and dreams. I respond appropriately to my yearnings, acting ethically and forthrightly for my own best interests.

cℰ

THE UNIVERSE GIFTS ME WITH COURAGE IN ALL THINGS

I cherish my own courage. I salute myself for the brave action I undertake in my life. I focus with clarity and appreciation on the choices I have made which have required courage and self-determination. I applaud myself for my strength and my daring. Rather than belittle myself for my fears, I choose to honor myself for the bravery with which I have often walked through my fears. I count back in specific ways and enumerate for myself examples of my own courage: the new friendship I have undertaken, the steadiness I have shown in a difficult job, the honesty I have displayed in opening a difficult conversation. I honor myself for my bigheartedness in the face of challenges from which I could have—but did not—shrunk back. My courage brings blessings to my life. My courage blesses the lives of others.

Very often people don't so much doubt their guidance as their
ability to follow it. This is where friends, the right kind
of friends, come in. "Trust yourself," these friends say.
"Try it and see what happens.
Maybe your guidance is right."

SONIA CHOQUETTE

‿

FRIENDSHIP BLESSES
AND FULFILLS ME

I cherish the committed friendship of those who have extended themselves on my behalf. I count myself lucky to have the support and encouragement of my friends. Rather than focus on the lacks in my friendships, I turn my perception instead to appreciating the many ways in which my friends have been loyal and even courageous in relationship to me. I enumerate for myself the times that I have felt a friend's courage in speaking a difficult truth. I count with gratitude the times friends have listened to me as I struggled to clarify an issue which was difficult for me to face.

Rather than look at the ways in which I feel I have been let down or betrayed, I choose today to focus on the ways in which I have been nurtured, encouraged, and protected.

The more faithfully you listen to the voice within you,

the better you will hear what is sounding outside.

And only she who listens can speak.

DAG HAMMARSKJÖLD

❦

THE UNIVERSE TEACHES ME
WITH GENTLE LOVE

Spirit mentors me with care and accuracy. As I open my heart and my hand to be counseled, I am partnered by divine wisdom. It is a great blessing that I do not walk alone. I am not without guidance. In every day, in every moment, there is a source of divine guidance available to me if I will turn within. Within me, I carry God. Within God, I am carried. There is no separation, only the forgetting of union. As I realize, accept, and appreciate my union with divinity, all things unfold for me more clearly. As I accept the grace within my current circumstances, my grace increases and flows forward to prepare my future. My life is a life of abundant blessings. My heart is a home for grace and good. As I cherish the gifts which accompany me now, I see greater gifts, greater love still unfolding. As I open my eyes to see and my ears to hear, I find the beauty of life is dazzling. This green planet, this garden, returns to grace as I am guided to husband it as carefully as I would my child. Graced and protected by higher forces, acutely attuned to higher goods, I protect and shepherd this planet to deepened health. My guidance blesses me and all I touch.

The truth is that this world is full of love. This world is an
embodiment of the bliss of God. Look at the trees—
God's love is vibrating in them. Look at the water—
God's love is vibrating in water. Look at the faces
of all the people—God's love is vibrating there.

SWAMI MUKTANANDA

&

MY LIFE IS A TREASURE CHEST AND I COUNT ITS WORTH

The life which I have now is rich and beautiful, intricate and valuable. I cherish the abundance which has come to my door. I take the time and attention to focus on the precise components of my life which please me. I notice the beauty of my surroundings, the harmony of my friendships, the synergy of the many parts working together to form a greater whole. I survey the life that I have created with fondness. I pause and appreciate the many small gifts which have brought me delight and renewal. Through the act of consciously cherishing what I do have, I open the doorway to even greater abundance. Allowing the changes in my life to build one upon the other, I allow a transformation in my needs and wants to coexist with appreciation for what I have wanted and have loved. Life is an evolutionary process. Each larger form is built upon the form from which it moves beyond. Recognizing this, I hold tenderness in my heart for both my past and my present. I allow my future to unfold, organically rooted in the soil of all I have been. I bless the treasure of my own unfolding.

☙

I GROW WITH NATURAL GRACE

I cherish the pace which God provides for my growth. I accept the tempo of God's action as appropriate to my native interests. Taking my cue from the seasons, I count my blessings in the small daily events which mark my calendar. What one small thing did I notice today that was filled with beauty? What small thing did I do today which expressed love? Rather than seeking always to have a life flooded by abundance, I turn to cherishing what I do have and husbanding it with care and gratitude. Rather than focusing on what more I would like to have, I focus on what I can do better to honor and respect that which I do have. I cherish my precise point of growth.

Go confidently in the direction of your dreams! Live the life
you've imagined. As you simplify your life, the laws
of the universe will be simpler.

&

I AM THE DREAM OF GOD
DREAMING GOD

I am a dreamer of divine dreams. The dreams of my heart are dreams which God fulfills for me. As I yearn, my prayer is heard and the answer is prepared. My every thought, my every action, is a moment in which divine support comes to me. I am never alone, never an exile, never a stranger from the heart of God. The heart of God holds me within its bountiful soil. I blossom there, rooted in faith, fed by the nutrients of divine love. As I source myself in God, as I draw my strength from divine abundance, divine supply, there is no lack, no shortcoming. Apparent delays and denials are truly detours which route me toward a higher good. I allow divine wisdom to alter and expand the dreams of my heart. I accept divine guidance, divine wisdom, and divine fulfillment. My dreams are good and goodness is the nature of God. My dreams, therefore, are God's. I go to God for their fulfillment.

We are scraps of iron. Your love is the magnet
that draws us near.

RUMI

❦

I AM A PARTICLE OF GOD
AND AN ARTICLE OF FAITH
IN ACTION

My destiny is unique and irreplaceable. My gifts and perceptions are powerful and important. My needs, goals, and desires are an outer manifestation of my inner divinity seeking to express itself for the good of all. As I realize my dreams I am an example to others that their dreams, too, have weight and consequence. As I harbor myself gently and birth my dreams carefully, I show by the respect with which I treat myself the respect with which all of us deserve to be treated. In acting toward myself in concrete and loving ways, I become ever more able to love others consciously and concretely. As I allow myself to receive good from my own hand, I also open myself to receiving good from others, giving them the gift of knowing that their love and contributions are felt by me as honored and important parts of my life. As I cherish myself, I cherish others as well. I am ever more loving, ever more heart-centered as I recognize that each of us desires and deserves a tender love which encourages us toward expansion. My active faith in the unique destiny of each of us blesses all I encounter with the gift of being truly, fully seen.

There are two aspects of individual harmony; the harmony
between body and soul, and the harmony between individuals.

HAZRAT INAYAT KHAN

ᚺ

MY FRIENDSHIPS ARE
A BEAUTIFUL HARVEST

I cherish the companions Spirit has given me. I honor those who share my life. I bless their talents, abilities, gifts, and personalities. I see them as divinely led, divinely placed in connection to me and to our mutual unfolding. Calling to mind that divinity resides within each of us, I regard all my relationships as sacred interactions, opportunities to experience Spirit in human form. Recognizing this, I draw on my own inner divinity to act with dignity and kindness, with harmony and grace. The spirit of universal love moves through me, to me, and out from me in all my connections. In every relationship, the heart of Spirit fills my heart with loving grace. I count my friendships as valued jewels. The hearts of my friends are my diamonds, emeralds, rubies, sapphires, and pearls. The unique gems of their personalities are their own divine spark. I cherish each for its beauty and richness.

The truth is that the inner Self of every human being is supremely great and supremely lovable. Everything is contained in the Self. The divine Principle that creates and sustains this world pulsates within us as our own Self. It scintillates in the heart and shines through all our senses.

SWAMI MUKTANANDA

CB

ALL OF HUMANITY IS MY BELOVED FAMILY

We are one tribe. I cherish our unity. We are united by our suffering and by our joy. One life flows through all life. One heart holds every heart. The loss I sustain today is the beginning of a larger, wiser, and kinder tomorrow. It is a part of the dignity of those we lose that we go forward bearing them as loving treasure in our hearts. I cherish those whom I carry in my heart. I honor their thoughts, their wisdom, their guidance, and their support. I bring them forward through my actions toward the future they empowered.

Every branch and leaf and fruit
reveals some aspect of God's
perfection: the cypress gives hint
of His majesty; the rose gives
tidings of His beauty.

JAMI

☙

I AM ONE WITH ALL THERE IS

I am connected to all of life. All of life blesses me with its connection. Even as I am able to value the beauty of a crystal, the radiance of a lily, the delicacy of a fern, so too am I beautiful and to be valued. As strong as an oak, as enduring in value as a rock formation, as intricate and individual as a snowflake, I am as consciously and as carefully created and crafted as any of these. Furthermore, I carry within me the co-creative powers to add to my beauty and my worth. As I chose to contribute to life, as I choose to consciously and creatively live to my fullest flowering, I become an expansion of the creator within me. This blesses all.

☙

I VOICE THE UNIVERSE
IN AN ORIGINAL WAY

I bring to life a unique and powerful voice. My insights and perceptions are important blessings. Voicing my insights and perceptions is important to the world. I am an irreplaceable individual whose gifts benefit all. Owning my gifts, inhabiting them, and expanding them are my gifts to the world and those with whom I share it. As I become larger, more colorful, and more truly myself, I create for others the realization that it is safe for them to become larger, more vibrant, more fully alive. Moving upward and outward in a spirit of creative community, I am non-competitive and truly collaborative, growing larger myself while helping others to achieve their true size as well. The cosmic web is alive with greater and greater consciousness, larger and brighter possibility.

As I extend my hand in my immediate world, I alter and enlarge the benevolence of the world as a whole. My every action is sweet and significant. Knowing this, I consciously and creatively act for the highest good. My unique voice and consciousness bless all.

We can smile, breathe, walk, and eat our meals in a way
that allows us to be in touch with the abundance of
happiness that is available. We are very good at preparing
to live, but not very good at living.

THICH NHAT HANH

MY HEART IS A GATEWAY FOR BLESSINGS TO UNFOLD

I celebrate the present abundance of my life. I enumerate and enjoy the many blessings which I do have and those I see now entering my life. I allow myself to count over the many dreams I have which have come true. I allow myself to enjoy the gifts which are already manifested in my experience. For example, I have friends who are loyal and true, whose conversation and companionship cheer me. This is a deep blessing and one which I remember to cherish. In my home, I have objects whose beauty brings me delight whenever I gaze on them. I am able even years after the acquisition to enjoy the grace and artistry with which beautiful objects have been made. On a seasonal level, new sights and sounds fill my life with delight: birds nest, breezes stir, the scent of flowers perfumes the air. For these many blessings, I give thanks. As I bless the abundance I do enjoy, I open my heart's capacity to receive even more.

Your words create what you speak about.
Learn to speak positively.

SANAYA ROMAN

☙

I REST IN
ABUNDANT SUPPLY

There are many doors through which my abundance comes to me. I bless them all. I am careful to allow many avenues for my good to flow to me. Rather than focus on one person or event as the sole source of my opportunity, I allow the universe to source me from myriad people and events. I open myself deeply and fully to the fact that I am held and embraced by an interactive universe. I am able to trigger my good by triggering good for others. As I concentrate on positive outflow, abundant inflow comes to me. I am sustained. I am expanded. I am prospered and blessed.

I create my own security by trusting the process of life.

LOUISE L. HAY

⬥

I AM SAFE AND SECURE

The heart of God holds all in safety. In times of separation from those I love, I remind myself that all of us are held safely in the heart of God. I ask God to touch those I love with healing grace and compassion. I ask God to gently guide those I love to their highest good and sweetest outcomes. While I long for physical contact with those I love, I remind myself that we are always in touch in spirit and that I touch them directly with grace whenever I pray for their happiness and well-being. Asking God to act for me, I pray for abundant blessings to those I love.

All nature is at the disposal of mankind.

We are to work with it.

Without it we cannot survive.

HILDEGARD OF BINGEN

I BLOOM IN THE
GARDEN OF GOD

God is the divine gardener and all souls bloom in divine love. As a green shoot welcomes the sun, I welcome the gardening hand of God. All souls are equal. All souls are rooted in God's soil. I am both a gardener and a flower blooming in the field of God. As a gardener, I ask that my hands be capable and gentle. I ask that I bring to the world beauty and tenderness, love and appreciation. As a part of the very garden which I tend, I ask that I flower fully, showing myself in my greatest beauty. I ask that I unfold perfectly, that my nature be a delight to those around me. Knowing my need for nutrients and care, I allow myself to be nurtured, shaped, and sheltered by those who care for me. In the blossoming of humankind, I gladly take my place as both a beauty and a caretaker of beauty. Humbled by the glory of the natural world, I bless the garden which contains us all.

I learned that the real creator was my inner Self,
the Shakti. . . . That desire to do something
is God inside talking through us.

<small>MICHELE SHEA</small>

☙

MY HEART IS HOME TO
PEACEFUL EXPANSION

I am a field resting in the sun. My dreams germinate and grow within the security of divine love. Grace dreams with me and through me. All of my dreams are divine in origin. All of my dreams are divinely fulfilled. As I reside in grace and grace resides in me, my endeavors are shaped and secured by the action of loving grace in the world. As I honor the promptings of my heart, I honor the heart of the universe. My wishes, goals, and desires are divinely sheltered, divinely inspired, divinely protected. Resting in divine power, they are harmonious in their unfolding; their unfolding is pivotal to the working-out of the greater good. Secure in universal power, my dreams and passions find powerful pathways to manifestation as grace births them to prosper in this world. I am peace expanding.

☙

I WALK IN PEACE

I walk in peace. Adversity melts away as I remember the spiritual
reality underlying all things. I claim my right to divine comfort, divine harmony. I release all apparent discord into the healing care of the universe, trusting completely in the larger good
that is unfolding. Divine calm centers my heart in its loving presence. I relax. Remembering I am sourced in divine protection, I
breathe in contentment and well-being. I am held in the heart of
God. All things work toward the good. As I embrace my part in
a larger and holier whole, that whole embraces me. This unity is
a great blessing which brings peace and comfort to my heart.

ॐ

I AM IN THE CENTER
OF GOD'S LOVE

The heart of God knows no distance. I am held and cherished in the heart of God. I am safe, protected, and companioned at all times. There is no place or circumstance in which I am alone, without divine company and counsel. In times of loneliness, I remind myself that God infuses all things: the chair, the table, the rug, the flower, the vase. Divinity flows through all life and is all life. My fingertips contain God. God is at my fingertips at all times. When I feel loneliness, fatigue, or despair, I comfort myself by knowing I am contained within the heart of God and if I will only look for God within my own heart, I will find both of us there.

Just remain in the center, watching.
And then forget that you are there.

LAO-TZU

❦

I AM IMMERSED
IN DIVINE LIFE

The river of God flows through my experience. My life is sourced in universal life. My gifts come to me from Spirit. Drawing upon Spirit, I live my life fully and joyously. I encounter difficulty with resiliency. I encounter adversity with faith. Sourced in Spirit, gifted by Spirit, I am enough, more than enough, for any calamity. Rooted in Spirit, my soul is wealthy. Help and companions come to me in troubled times. I draw upon Spirit as I would a deep, clear, and pure stream of healing water. Dipping my heart into the flow of faith, I emerge refreshed and energized despite the severity of the hardships which I encounter. Spirit blesses my life.

If anything is sacred, the human body is sacred.

WALT WHITMAN

☙

MY HEALTH IS ROOTED
IN GOD

I honor the physical gift of health with which God has graced me. I give thanks for my vitality, my clarity, my vibrancy. Drawing strength from my connection to the natural world, I allow the physical vehicle of my body to be cherished and loved. Rather than focusing on what I wish were different, I focus instead on the loving loyalty and service which my body has so freely given me. Rather than say, "I wish this part of me were different," I instead say, "I am grateful that this part of me is exactly as it is." There is at least one feature of mine which I can wholly cherish: my eyes, my nose, my hair, my hands, feet, or shoulders. Today I willingly and positively focus on the beauty of the physical form which I have been given.

Our physical body possesses a wisdom which we who inhabit
the body lack. We give it orders which make no sense.

Henry Miller

ॐ

MY BODY IS MY TEACHER
AND MY GUIDE

My body is more than a vehicle which carries me through life. My body is a storehouse for my memories, a sensitive radar kit which warns me of danger, a wise teacher who signals me how best to care for my spirit. When I listen to my body, I am led into right and wise actions. When I take seriously the guidance it offers, I make decisions which honor me in a holistic way.

My body grounds me and protects me. My body is sacred and as knowing as a temple oracle. Often the intuitive warnings of my body regarding people, places, and events are the deepest safety I am given. I bless my body for its loyal surveillance on my behalf. I bless my body for its patient endurance, its mercurial intuition, and its persistence in speaking to me even when I slough aside the guidance it bears. My body is the most loyal of my friends. I bless my body for its loyal companionship and commit to regarding it with tender care.

I wish to exchange this flash-of-lightning faith for
continuous daylight, this fever-glow for a benign climate.

RALPH WALDO EMERSON

⁓

MY LIFE IS VALUABLE
AND INTERESTING

I value my sense of history. I am alert to the many colorful and enjoyable episodes in my own life's unfolding. Rather than bemoan a lack of color or adventure in my life, I consciously choose to notice and appreciate the many small adventures and victories which each of my days entertains. I focus on the precise and measurable evidence of good that comes to me as I am alert to life's many blessings. I notice, remark, and remember the kind word, the well-told joke, the flashing beauty of a small finch lighting on a roadside shrub. Alert to the beauty and detail around me, I revel ever more fully in the many graces life has to offer me.

Prayer is an attitude of the heart.

❦

MY HEART BRIMS WITH
AFFECTION AND EXPANSION

I am committed to gratitude in my life. This choice opens my perceptions to receive my good. This choice shows me the inner doorway through which abundance comes to me. My heart is connected to universal love. Opening to my inner connection to Source, I receive an inflow of love and further gratitude. I give out an outflow of love and further gratitude. Gratitude for me is active. It is an inner decision to name and cherish what I love. It is a recognition of the many ways in which I myself am loved and cherished. In committed gratitude, I strive to touch all with the loving-kindness which touches me. I practice the principles of love in action. I am kind and compassionate first to myself and then to all others. I cherish our worth, our dignity, our shared path as co-creative beings shaping our shared world.

My heart holds within it every form,

it contains a pasture for gazelles,

a monastery for Christian monks.

IBN ARABI

☙

I CELEBRATE THE UNITY
OF ALL LIFE

One life runs through everything. The oak, the elm, the ash, my own body, the dove, the doe, the ox—all are creatures of one life. Rooted in this knowledge, I live carefully and consciously. I bless all creatures and all elements of this earth. I live in harmony. I live with grace. I walk humbly and in friendship with all that lives. I open my heart to the teachings of all of life. I learn from water, from soil, from budding growth. I learn from harvest, from decline, and from decay. I embrace the cycles of the living world. I take my place on the wheel of life. I lead and I follow. I partner and am partnered. I accept the grace and companionship of all with whom I share this earth. I bless the unity of life.

Because he believes in himself,
he doesn't try to convince others.
Because he is content with himself,
he doesn't need others' approval.
Because he accepts himself,
the whole world accepts him.

TAO-TE CHING

⌘

MY SOUL IS
A DIVINE COMPANION

I count myself fortunate to be my own companion on life's journey. I am interested by my thoughts and perceptions. I am conscious of the many gifts I bring to living: my stamina, my humor, my perceptivity, my integrity. I count myself lucky to be responsible for my unfolding. I appreciate my commitment to being personally responsible for the caliber of my life, for undertaking an active role in the quality of my own life. I applaud my ability to act decisively on my own behalf, to seek out persons and activities which are of interest to me. I remind myself that I am lucky indeed to have someone of my own caliber as my constant friend, my loyal ally. Rather than berate myself for shortcomings or imagined flaws, I cherish the many parts of my character which make me a pleasure in my own life.

Let your heart's light guide you to my house.
Let your heart's light show you that we are one.

☙

LOYALTY IS MY GIFT
AND MY LANTERN

I esteem myself for my loyalty. I recognize that my capacity to commit and continue in relationships has been an invaluable part of what has brought richness and continuity to my life. I commend myself for the willingness I have displayed to work through differences with those I love. I honor myself for my stamina in challenging emotional situations. I appreciate my ability to allow differences to be aired, recognized, and worked through. I value my capacity for undertaking the responsibility of long-term relationships. I salute the part of me which has the maturity and compassion to allow myself and others to expand and evolve. I bless my lantern-heart and allow it to light my path.

*You must remember that man is noble, man is sublime, man
is divine, and can accomplish whatever he desires.*

SWAMI MUKTANANDA

⁂

MY STRENGTH
IS A FORTRESS

I cherish the depths of my inner resources. I have far more stamina, resiliency, and power than I sometimes know. Counting my true reservoirs of inner potency, I see that I am strong—stronger than I know, even stronger than I need. Every power that I need to meet my life is a power which is already contained within me. I am funded in universal strength. Claiming that power to be my bedrock and my birthright, I meet adversity with calm fortitude. I bless my strength. I bless the security that it provides.

I WALK IN SPIRITUAL BEAUTY

Divine presence is the foundation of my life. It is solid and unshakable. It is permanent, eternal, and always present. I am the recipient of great goodwill. This goodwill is timeless and unchanging. There is a benevolent force which intends me good and expansion. I receive blessings from many quarters. My good comes to me from all directions and at all times. I rest in divine love as my fortress. I am surrounded by good. Good upholds me and is my strength. In all my endeavors, in all my affairs, good unfolds and prospers me. Good blesses all of my relationships. My spirit and my life are one with the benevolent force of the universe.

If the Angel deigns to come it will be because you have
convinced her, not by tears but by your humble resolve,
to be always willing to be a beginner.

DIVINE GUIDANCE SPEAKS
WITHIN ME AND
THROUGH THE WORLD

Divine love guides me. I count—and I count on—this blessing. Reminding myself that Spirit always speaks both to
me and through me, I listen with my heart and I hear with clarity. In every situation, I find the path of compassion, the voice of
higher wisdom. I am able to hear divine guidance. I seek my inner
wisdom and it comes to me. It is always there. There is a right solution, a good outcome for every difficulty. The world evolves in
all its particulars toward higher good and harmony. I am able to
be a part of this upward evolution as I listen and respond to my
inner cues. I do not need to act out of fear. I do not need to force

solutions. My inner wisdom guides me. As I listen to my heart, I find support in the outer world. There is no place too isolated for guidance to reach me through inner and outer promptings. I ask to be led. I listen within me and without. The world responds to my listening with a voice of compassion and clear guidance. I am blessed by the guidance I receive.

Life is sacred. Life is art. Life is sacred art.

GABRIELLE ROTH

&

MY LIFE IS A JEWEL BOX
OF PRECIOUS MOMENTS

When I count and encounter my blessings, I experience a sense of fullness, safety, and satisfaction. I have enough. My heart is bountiful. My life is dowried by rich companions and rewarding experiences. As I experience the power and goodness of the universe, I experience my own power and goodness. I experience that I am enough—more than enough. I experience flow, increased flow and expanded flow. Opening to receive this flow, I become larger and more magnificent. I am part of a grand and glorious design. A grand and glorious design is part of me. I celebrate the grandeur of this fact with a humble heart.

In the garden every flower
Has its purpose and its hour—
The tulip and delphinium,
To only name a minimum.

"AVALON," JULIA CAMERON

DIVERSITY IS RAINBOW-HUED
IN MY EXPERIENCE

Mine is a multicolored life. It is rich in its differences, rewarding in its rich and variable components. My friendships, my interests, travels, and my pursuits bring me a world of variety, a wealth of differing goods. While grounded in my individual life, I am privileged to share the colorful lives of many. My explorations culturally, intellectually, and spiritually bring to me the riches from many horizons, the bounty of many lands. I embrace diversity in my life. I accept it, invite it, and enjoy it.

We know how to sacrifice ten years for a diploma, and we
are willing to work very hard to get a job, a car, a house,
and so on. But we have difficulty remembering that we are
alive in the present moment, the only moment there is for us
to be alive. Every breath we take, every step we make, can be
filled with peace, joy, and serenity. We need only to be
awake, alive in the present moment.

THICH NHAT HANH

I WELCOME JOY AS MY
SPIRITUAL COMPANION

I invite joy to bless my life. I welcome joy to my heart. Asceticism, hardship, grandiosity—these are enemies, not the handmaidens of spiritual growth. Gentleness, opening attention—these are the gardening tools which best encourage growth. In every moment, I can choose between will and willingness, between determination and fructification. As I allow myself to be rendered gently fruitful, I become fluid from moment to moment. The harshness of my experience slips away. Spirituality requires vulnerability and openness. As I still myself rather than "steel" myself, I hear ever more clearly the quiet promptings of inner growth. As I follow the lead which joy sets in my life, I am gently, safely, and surely led.

We are told that prayer brings angels down. But if prayer is thought, concentrated and distilled, the clear, pure yearning of the heart, is prayer itself also the manifestation of the divine? The desire itself being granted as a gift of God, in order that its satisfaction may be given us by God?

Sophy Burnham

ॐ

I AM SECURE IN THE FLOW OF GRACEFUL GOOD

I anticipate the blessings hidden in all circumstances. Therefore, I surrender my need to control relationships and events. I open my heart to divine outcomes, divine timing. I allow my agendas to become divine agendas. I allow the forms and functions of people and situations to unfold naturally to the highest good. Guided by grace and guarded by grace, the people and circumstances of my life flow into shapes which benefit everyone. I allow Spirit to shape my life into ever more satisfying forms. I invite Spirit to counsel me on how I can best cooperate with, rather than control, the graceful unfolding of my good.

Committed to accepting specific suggestions in all circumstances, knowing that Spirit is precise and particular, I accept the guidance of God: good, orderly direction. I surrender my resistance to the action of grace in my endeavors. I open my heart to the creative input of higher realms. I allow divine guidance to enter and act in my affairs, moving and shaping the events of my life into ever more perfect forms, ever more tangible blessings. The action of grace is concrete and substantial. As I invite the action of grace into my life, my blessings are guaranteed.

Respect is love. The heart is also love—and so are you.

SWAMI CHIDVILASANANDA

☙

MY WORLD IS FILLED
WITH GRACEFUL LOVE

My path is broad and gentle. Ours is a journey of shared hearts. I remind myself that I am blessed with friendship, gifted with acquaintances and associations who travel with me toward the highest good. Reminding myself, always, that we are all traveling together, I develop my individuality while welcoming the individuality of others. As much as I yearn to be truly seen and truly loved, I seek to see others truly and truly love them. I offer to those I encounter a believing mirror. I reflect back to them their dignity, their beauty, their potential and divine spark. Treating all whom I encounter with respect and affection, I allow my heart to be a vessel for healing love. Drawing on universal love to love through me, I love freely and without fatigue. I open my heart to actualizing grace in each encounter.

I allow Spirit to enter my interactions, shaping them and leavening them to a richer bread. I am nourished by Spirit and through Spirit. I seek to bless and nourish others by expressing Spirit through me.

We should always remember:
God reveals Himself to us within us in the form of love.

❦

I WITNESS THE GOOD IN
OTHERS AND CELEBRATE
THEIR GROWTH

The growth of one blesses all. I am committed to grow in love. All that I touch, I leave in love. I move through this world consciously and creatively. I act with quiet authority moving from my heart to touch the dreams and hearts of others. As I faithfully mirror to others their worth and their precious and irreplaceable individuality, I myself play an irreplaceable part in bringing the world to greater abundance. So often all that is needed is an act of loving attendance. I marshal myself to offer that witness. In witnessing others in their passage I ratify the importance of my own. Life is led both individually and collectively. I honor my importance and the importance of others. None of us is dispensable, none of us is replaceable. In the chorus of life

237

each of us brings a True Note, a perfect pitch which adds to the harmony of the whole. I act creatively and consciously to actively endorse and encourage the expansion of those whose lives I touch. Believing in the goodness of each, I add to the goodness of all. We bless each other even in passing.

New, wonderful experiences now enter my life.
I am safe.

LOUISE LILTAY

I WELCOME THE ARRIVAL
OF NEW LOVES

I give thanks for my new friendships. I welcome my new loves, my new acquaintances. Knowing that we have intersected as part of a higher plan, I extend my heart and my hand to new people and new events, welcoming them home to their place in my world. Rather than live in a closed, insular, and distanced manner, I fling open the doors to my heart. My life is a courtyard filled by the sun. My courtyard is peopled by those I love and those whom I am learning to love. I bless my capacity to love. My capacity to love blesses me.

It would be good to find some quiet inlet where the waters
were still enough for reflection, where one might sense
the joy of the moment, rather than plan breathlessly
for a dozen mingled treats in the future.

KATHLEEN NORRIS

MY LIFE IS A WELLSPRING
OF GRACE

I am sourced in divine flow. It pours out from me, shaped by me uniquely, to bless my world. My spiritual essence matters to me and others. As I am true to myself, I am true to others. I am divinely led and guided in all my dealings. Trusting in this, I offer others the safety of honest companionship, the reality of grounded love. Drawing on God source, my love is pure and healing. It is divine water for a thirsty world. I bless the flow which flows through me. This flow blesses my world.

What a piece of work is a man! How noble in reason!
how infinite in faculties! in form and moving how
express and admirable! in action how like an angel!
in apprehension how like a god!

WILLIAM SHAKESPEARE

෨

I AM UNIQUE
AND IRREPLACEABLE

My personality, with all its quirks, foibles, and eccentricities, is a perfect expression of God energy moving into the world. I cherish my individual expression of divine life. I acknowledge that I am uniquely designed to bring certain energies into play in an innovative and beneficial way for all. There is something in my own creative makeup that is necessary to the good of the world. I am designed specifically to make a unique and meaningful contribution. There is a beauty and a purpose to my precise personality. I am not an accident, a mistake, or a haphazard collection of influences. I am a self-evolving and important energy which brings to the world a precise and important healing medicine. My influence and impact on others is a matter of large consequence. Believing this is not a matter of ego. It is a recognition of the divine plan which embraces us all. I am a pivotal and important part of this plan. My actions and attitudes have weight and consequence. As I consciously and creatively come into my full flowering, I bring the best and the brightest of myself as blessings into the world.

༄

I EXPAND MY HEART
IN THE SAFETY OF
SPIRITUAL PROTECTION

I commit myself to the blessing of self-expansion. I am a part of a larger whole, but that larger whole is also a part of me. I can expand or contract my consciousness according to my openness and receptivity. As I harbor feelings of disappointment and betrayal, I block the flow of my larger good. As I clear the air by acknowledging the wounds I have allowed to dampen my faith, I enter a fuller and more firmly based relationship with my larger self. I therefore commit myself to fully facing and feeling the complicated emotions that arise within me as I move through my world. Choosing to be intimate first to myself and to God and then to others, I commit to staying current with myself and with my companions. Through this commitment, I allow life to flow through me like a river. Its flow washes me clear of debris while bearing to me the silt for richer growth. I accept the blessing of my own expansive nature.

Satisfaction of one's curiosity is one of the greatest
sources of happiness in life.

<small>LINUS PAULING</small>

෧

MY MIND IS NOURISHED
BY DIVINE IDEAS

I count myself lucky to have the opportunities which surround me for intellectual fulfillment. I count with delight the ways in which my life is enriched by the resources which are at hand. Rather than focus on what is lacking, I choose today to enumerate the things which do interest and delight me. I count the areas in which I have abundant resources. I am grateful for the diversity of my friends and my community. Choosing to see that I can play an increasingly accurate role in my own self-nurturance, I recognize the many as yet untapped arenas for self-enrichment with which I am supplied. It is a matter of perception whether I choose to view my life as half-filled and able to be ever more abundant or half-empty and ever more disappointing. Recognizing that the choice is mine, I turn my focus toward the ways in which I can deepen and expand my mind and my spirit. My mind is blessed by the food of my intellectual interests.

❧

MY TENACITY IS A POWERFUL ENGINE FOR GOOD

I am blessed by my own tenacity. I contain an inner reservoir of gritty strength, which serves me and others well. My capacity to stick to a commitment is a safe and trustworthy component of my character. My tenacity is the building block for my successful career, relationship, family life, and friendships.

Obstacles test me but they do not deter me. I am able, always, to tap an inner resilient strength which serves me. Even when life is a desert, I find my careful way. Like a camel, I carry within myself stamina and the wisdom to use my energy wisely for the long trek. I am a creature of miraculous endurance. My will and my grounded passion form the basis for my tenacious movement through life. I bless my tenacity for its important, unsung heroism.

It is said that desire is a product of the will, but the
converse is in fact true: will is a product of desire.

DENIS DIDEROT

MY WILL IS A POWERFUL
ENERGY USED FOR GOOD

I bless the steely temper of my will. The steel of my resolve graces me with tenacity, blesses me with endurance, and assures me of success. My will is a potent force which carries me in the direction of good. As I set my will on worthy objectives and goals, as I focus my will and act in accordance with its desires, I find myself moving effectively and powerfully in the world. My will is rooted in divine guidance and expressed as right action. My will is a sword that cuts away difficulties and defends the values I cherish. I bless my will for its very willingness to bless me.

If we are not fully ourselves, truly in
the present moment, we miss everything.

ॐ

I LIVE IN THE POWER
OF THE MOMENT

Every moment is a power point for creative choice. This realization is a great blessing. Knowing this, I choose to live my life consciously and concretely, moment by moment, choosing attitudes and actions which cause my life to flourish and expand. I am an arrow shot through time. My consciousness carries my accumulated energy and wisdom. As I allow my fullest self to choose my thoughts and behaviors, I act creatively and expansively. My rich life becomes richer still. I am alert to inner and outer promptings which cause me to recognize and respond to my ever-increased opportunities, my ever-increased blessings. As I create for myself an inner expectation of enlarged goodness and potential, my life becomes adventurous, optimistic, and expansive. In each moment, I choose the highest good, the clearest path, the most open-hearted perspective. Each choice, each moment blesses me. I count my good fortune at every turn.

❧

THE EARTH IS MY JOY
AND COMFORT

The earth consoles me in all things. In times of grief, I turn to the natural world. I allow the earth to comfort me. I study the lesson of cyclicality. I see the place of death in life. Faced with loss, I seek comfort in the heart of loss. In every loss, at its very heart, is the gift of life. When I am tempted by despair, I look more closely at the face of grief. I see its dignity, its humanity. I see that I am part of a larger whole. There is no loss which is new to this earth. There is no grief which is larger than life. The most grievous loss, the most devastating catastrophe—at its heart even this grief is embraced by a compassionate earth. I bless the heart of this green planet which cradles us all.

❧

THE ANIMAL KINGDOM
BLESSES MY LIFE

Even in the midst of the city, I find daily contact with animals that cheer me and help me to put my life into perspective. I bless the companionship of all animals as they cross my path: the calico cat sitting in the window above the window box of pansies; the white dove flying with its darker sisters as I pass the gothic hulk of a city church; the sunny spaniel strolling at its owner's side on a city street—all of these creatures light my heart and remind me of my own animal nature.

Animals have the gift of living in the moment. They inhabit their physical world with attention and grace. Taking a cue from their presence, I learn the lesson of attention, the blessing of alert focus on the world around me.

Chance is always powerful. Let your hook be always cast;
in the pool where you least expect it, there will be a fish.

OVID

MY LIFE IS SHAPED BY DIVINE GUIDANCE TO GREATER BEAUTY

I open myself to the freedom of change. I bless the changes which come to me. Trusting in change, I relax my grip on the contours of my life. I allow new beginnings. I allow alteration, accommodation, change. I invite the interaction of imagination and possibility. I surrender agendas, outlines, plots. Recognizing that life is both active and interactive, I hold out my hand to dance, knowing that I am partnered more variably and creatively than I can yet conceive. I bless the changeable creativity of life in its unfolding.

It is not because things are difficult that we do not dare;
it is because we do not dare that they are difficult.

SENECA

With courage you will dare to take risks,
have the strength to be compassionate and the
wisdom to be humble. Courage is the
foundation of integrity.

KESHAVEN NAIR

THE UNIVERSE FUNDS
ME WITH POWER
AND PROTECTION

I am a power to be reckoned with. I salute my capacity to act. My choices and decisions, my attitudes and actions shape the world in which I live. Sourced in God, I have tremendous resources which I can marshal for good. As I pass through every day, my respect and receptivity to others help determine the caliber of world which we share. There is no moment in which I cannot make a positive contribution. By my choices and my concrete and personal actions, I directly impact the lives of all with whom I deal. My smile, my concerned question, my joke or gaiety, these impact not only those with whom I interact but also all those with whom they interact. My consciousness is a fountain of good. As I pour forth positive energy, I change the world. Life is made of small moments which have a large impact. My positive belief and support can help to change the trajectory of a lifetime. As I mirror to others their true value and worth, I create a world in which all of us are more truly valued. I bless with dignity all those I encounter.

Truly it is in the darkness that one finds the light, so when
we are in sorrow, then this light is nearest all of us.

MEISTER ECKHART

ᴄᴈ

I ACCEPT MY LOSS AS THE GATEWAY TO GAIN

The universe gives to me by what it takes away. My loss is a gain which I am as yet unable to see. As I let go of the good to which I cling, other good moves toward me. As I surrender my shortsighted agenda, events and people better suited to my long-term happiness enter my life. In the face of loss, I feel my feelings but I do not draw conclusions based on false evidence appearing real. I remind myself that life is evolutionary, that situations have a way of working toward my good if I will stand aside in faith and allow the hand of the universe to set things right. I bless the grace active in my life which carries all things toward the good.

*I turn to the Presence of God at the center of my being and
it is here that I discover the nature of the Good which must
and does reside in the back of all people and events.*

ERNEST HOLMES

☙

ADVERSITY IS
MISPERCEPTION AS ALL
WORKS TOWARD THE GOOD

I bless my perceived rival. I affirm my inner worth regardless of outcome. I affirm, too, the inner worth of my perceived rival. Knowing all works together for the good, I claim for each of us the highest good. I expect the working-out of our difficulties to create the best path for each of us. Knowing that no one person can block my good, I surrender my sense of adversity. There is enough good for all. Each of us is prospered by and through each other. My perceived rival is a means to my achieving a good end. I bless my disguised friend.

In the middle of difficulty lies opportunity.

ALBERT EINSTEIN

☙

MY HEART IS A GATEWAY
FOR GOD

My faith is a lantern in times of darkness, a gentle hearth against the cold. My response to loss is faith. My response to a door which closes is anticipation of another, more appropriate, door opening. As I release my insistence on having my good come to me from the persons and situations which I myself select, I open myself to greater good which comes to me from more persons and more sources than I can yet imagine. The universe is abundant in its desires for me. There is a plan and a perfect pace for my blossoming and unfolding. In the face of loss, I feel my feelings and I accept them. That done, I respond next with curiosity. What new plans does the universe have for me? What new person is meant to enter my life now? The flow of life is a river filled with opportunity. I allow that river to gift me with riches, to wash away my regrets, my doubts, my despair. In every loss, I see the beginning of a new unfolding. As I accept my loss, I ready myself for the hidden gift which it contains. Rather than close my heart defensively, I open my heart as a wide gate for the blessings of the world to enter.

When you really listen to yourself, you can heal yourself.

CEANNE DEROHAN

&

THE LAMP OF INNER WISDOM LIGHTS MY PATH

I recognize that I have a gift for insight. I salute myself for being willing to listen to my inner wisdom. I honor myself for my willingness to hold true to what I perceive even when my perceptions are not shared by those around me. In this way, I value and support my own individuality. I recognize that my perceptions are unique and trustworthy. I count my insight as a powerful blessing in my life and in the lives of those with whom I am intimate. I am tender toward myself regarding the vulnerability which my insights may engender as I willingly let go of denial and rigid and doctrinaire thinking, which is a barrier to my perceiving the truth. I bless the ever-expanding light I have to see by.

Patience is the companion of wisdom.

ST. AUGUSTINE

&

MY LIFE UNFOLDS
IN SPIRIT'S TIME

I bless Spirit's timing in my life. I surrender my sense of drama and urgency. I recognize that the slower seasons of life are necessary to find my showier and more rapid periods of expansion. I surrender my need for life to be filled with large and dramatic moments. I accept small gains, small victories. Turning away from the idea that there is some "quick fix" which will make me feel heroic and invulnerable, I accept the fact that I am a worker among workers, a friend among friends. In choosing not to force the pace of my life, I embrace wisdom over velocity.

If you read the scriptures and the philosophies, three terms
recur constantly: humility, purity, and self-control.
They say if you have these three, then you become
worthy of attaining the Truth.

SWAMI CHIDVILASANANDA

ⷮ

WISDOM GIVES PATIENCE
TO MY SOUL

My soul is a patient traveler. I am grateful for my patient soul. Despite the temptation to think and act rashly, I root myself in the goodness of Spirit and act with temperance and wisdom. I treat myself with gentle compassion when I find myself anxious or panicky due to imagined difficulties. At all times, in all places, I remind myself that Spirit is the source of my security and that when I rest in Spirit I rest in loving companionship. In times of loneliness, when I feel misunderstood and abandoned, I allow myself to feel the presence of Spirit, guiding and supporting me, holding me safe and secure despite my fears and misgivings. I bless the path I travel with spiritual safety.

We must stop planning, plotting, and scheming and let
Infinite Intelligence solve the problem in Its own way.
God-power is subtle, silent, and irresistible. It levels
mountains and fills in valleys and knows no defeat!
Our part is to prepare for our blessings and
follow our intuitive leads.

We now give Infinite Intelligence
right-of-way.

FLORENCE SCOVEL SHINN

THE UNIVERSE IS MY
PROTECTIVE PARENT

I am a cherished child of Spirit. I am worthy to receive my blessings. I am deserving of all the benefits and blessings which enter my life. I am good and good things come to me—good
people, good events, good opportunities, good lessons, good in
many and multiple forms. As I accept my good, it multiplies. As

I bless my good, it becomes mine in a harmonious and natural way. I enlarge my life and my life enlarges me. I expand gracefully and gently to encompass an ever more abundant life. I bless the circle of sacred safety within which I grow.

I acknowledge and declare that the Creator of all things
is now manifesting as perfection and harmony
in all my experiences.

ERNEST HOLMES

DIVINE TIMING
GUIDES MY LIFE

Divine timing guides my life. All events are unfolding for my highest good. As I seek divine will in every circumstance, I find peace, serenity, and right action. These are my blessings. I am able to enter into inner security even in the midst of outer turbulence. Reminding myself that there is an underlying flow of good in all events, I accept timing which at first may frustrate or confuse me. Knowing that I am grounded in spiritual reality, I am able to face life's circumstances with the wisdom of the long view. In every situation, the hand of grace is active for my good.

Your desire is your prayer. Picture the fulfillment of your
desire now and feel its reality and you will experience
the joy of the answered prayer.

Dr. Joseph Murphy

I SOFTEN MY HEART TO LOVE'S TOUCH

I accept the gift of my vulnerability. I am willing to be vulnerable to love. I am willing to reveal myself in all of my human beauty and frailty. I am willing to be as I am, both perfect and a work in progress. I am willing to be unfinished, unpolished, in a state of change. I am willing to accept myself as I am and I am willing to allow others to see me as I am. I am willing to be unveiled and undefended. I am willing to be seen and understood. I am willing to view myself and others with compassion. I am willing to view myself and others nonjudgmentally. I am willing to be the human being, complete in myself without the need for accomplishment to justify my worth. Blessing myself just as I am, I lovingly open to all I can be.

Every soul is a melody which needs renewing.

STÉPHANE MALLARMÉ

❦

MY HEARING
BRINGS ME NEWS

I bless my capacity to hear the world around me. My physical sense of sound connects me to my world. The rippling sound of water, the hushed whisper of the wind, the sigh of my lover's breath, the sweet sound of a Sunday choir—all these and more are gifts to me. I focus on the sounds my hearing brings to me. I learn discernment and compassion from the tones I encounter and respond to. My hearing is acute and accurate. I am able to respond with delicacy to the subtle undercurrents revealed to me through sound.

༄

I SAVOR MY SENSE
OF TASTE

I bless the physical gift of taste which enlivens my world. The
tart taste of raspberries, the gentle taste of milk, the subtlety
of spices, the crisp pungence of an apple—all flavors come to me
as gifts which I enjoy. My sense of taste brings me pleasure, comfort, and connection.

I take time to savor what I eat, to appreciate the distinct flavors
and exquisite shadings which food brings to my mouth. I bless my
appetite and I enjoy its satisfaction. The taste of the food I eat fills
me with gratitude. My life is delicious and I savor it.

Every flower is a soul blossoming in nature.

GÉRARD DE NERVAL

CB

MY SENSE OF SMELL
DEEPENS MY WORLD

The scent of newly mown grass, the smell of freshly baked bread, the aroma of pine boughs, the heady perfume of lilies—my world is filled with scents which bring me joy and comfort. The odor of freshly waxed wood, the scent of a baby's skin, the pungent smell of onions, the heady smell of autumn leaves— each of these scents brings to me a specific pleasure, a message of my benign connection to the world. I bless, too, the sense of safety conveyed to me by smell—the acrid scent of something burning, the odor of stale food that I should not eat. My sense of smell blesses me with good sense as well as with good scents.

In times of disquiet, I turn to scent to comfort me. I light a scented candle, burn a fragrant incense, mist myself with a perfume or drop of aromatic oil. My sense of smell connects me to a sense of well-being. I use it consciously and well.

☙

MY HEALTH IS A MIRROR
TO BRING ME CLARITY

In times of disease, I slow down, center myself, and focus on the blessing hidden within the circumstance. What am I meant to attend to? What grief have I ignored? What stress have I turned aside or buried? What blessing can be found by slowing down, by turning within? Disease begins as dis-ease. What can I do to ease my spirit? What blessing can I choose to encounter? A falling leaf, a spring flower, the soft drifting of a winter snow? Beautiful music, the smell of soup, the taste of a good piece of bread—all these speak to my heart, which has ears to hear them. The cleansing rain falls within as well as without. I open the ears and eyes of my heart to the abundant blessings of my natural world. I take my ease.

In a dark time, the eye begins to see.

THEODORE ROETHKE

ↈ

MY PLANS AND AGENDAS
ARE EXPANDED AND
CORRECTED BY THE
UNIVERSE

My life is blessed by grace—which acts with its own timing. In times of frustration, in times of fear, as loss and difficulty surround me, I release my plans and outcomes to the larger plans and outcomes unfolding for my benefit. Letting go of my insistence on immediate gratification, I relax into the better working-out of details and dimensions hidden from my view. Affirming that all works for the good of all if I open to the grace of cooperation, I open my heart to God's timing, God's wisdom, God's working-out of gentle benefits for all.

Listening is a form of accepting.

STELLA TERRILL MANN

I AM TEACHABLE AND HOLD
A BEGINNER'S HEART

I am willing to be guided and corrected. This attitude is a great blessing. I am willing to have my thinking, my attitudes, and my actions shaped by a wisdom higher than my own. Surrendering my impatience, my doubt, and my despair, I ask, in faith, for guidance to come to me. I resolve to be of good heart and to place my life in the care of higher forces which hold toward me a benevolent and protective view. I bless the humility which opens my heart to receiving help, care, and spiritual protection.

Finally I looked within my own heart and there
I found Him—He was nowhere else.

❦

MY HEART LISTENS TO
THE VOICE WITHIN

My heart is fulfilled. Its yearnings are prayers preparing to be answered. The good I am seeking seeks me as well. The love I wish for is mine as I love in return. It is the nature of Spirit to give. It is my nature to receive. As I go to Spirit to fulfill my desires, I recognize that Spirit is also the source of those desires. I am a creative being. The creator within me yearns for what it wants to create. As I open myself to the divine creative energy which flows through me, I am both the prayer and its answer.

It is man's foremost duty to awaken the understanding of
the inner Self and to know his own real inner greatness.
Once he knows his true worth, he can know the worth
of others. Therefore, meditate on your Self, honor and
worship your own Self, kneel to your own Self, and see
the Lord who is hidden in your own heart.

SWAMI MUKTANANDA

I AM BY NATURE
LOVABLE AND LOVED

I count myself as lovable. I do not need to control myself, patrol myself, or improve myself to be loved. Those who love me find me in their hearts. My lovability is not an issue. I accept the love that is offered to me and I rejoice in its appearance. I allow others to love as they are able in ways that may startle and delight me. I release my pictures of love and accept the variability of love. I allow the love in my life to be subtle, rigorous, many-colored, and multifaceted. I do not pursue love. I love by opening to love.

Committing your ways unto the Lord seems very difficult to
most people. It means, of course, to follow intuition,
for intuition is the magic path, the beeline to your
demonstration. Intuition is a Spiritual faculty above the intellect.
It is the "still small voice" commonly called a hunch,
which says, "this is the way, walk ye in it."

FLORENCE SCOVEL SHINN

I ENJOY MY OWN
COMPANIONSHIP

My solitude brings me the blessing of intimacy with myself. When I am alone, I explore my own companionship, learn my own thoughts, feelings, needs, and desires. Underneath my feelings of loneliness, I sense a deeper truth: that I am companioned by the universe, that periods of solitude are periods of learning as I cock my ear and heart for guidance from higher realms. I am constantly tutored, constantly spoken to, and guided by higher forces which are universal in nature and personal in expression. Though the universe is large, I am not so small that my presence isn't noted and counted. I contain the universe within me just as the universe contains me. When I appeal to higher forces, I am appealing to the best within myself. "Lo, I contain multitudes," the poet Walt Whitman remarked. In my times of solitude, I find joy in the multitudes I contain. I bless my own nature for its riches and diversity. I am my friend.

See the world as your self.

Have faith in the way things are.

Love the world as your self;

then you can care for all things.

Tao-te Ching

CB

MY HEART IS CHERISHED
AND SECURE

Today I cherish the security of a love returned. I have in my life those whose friendship and devotion are assured. I reach to them and they reach to me in return. We have each other's best interests at heart. We share each other's dreams and visions of a meaningful life. I am willing to commit myself to deep and loving friendships. I am willing to take into my heart the dreams and aspirations of those I love. I am willing to support them in their dreams' unfolding. I am willing to cheer, to console, to counsel, and not compete. Taking as my guidance the rule that everyone's good prospers everyone, I am able to be a generous friend, open to the happiness and fulfillment of my friends' dreams and wishes. I am secure in the fact that as one of us moves forward we all move forward. I am able to extend myself in faith knowing I am equally and fully supported in return. As I put positive energy into the universe, the universe returns to my energy in kind.

I PRACTICE OPTIMISM AS
A CONSCIOUS CHOICE

In times of loss and difficulty, I choose to consciously deepen
my strength through actively seeking the blessing hidden in
my adversity. I do not deny my painful feelings or run from them
but I do choose to move through them, seeking the opportunity
for insight that lies for me on the other side. I do not suffer for
the sake of suffering or mistake pain as the only soil for my
spiritual growth. Instead, I remind myself that suffering and pain
are temporary while my spiritual comfort is eternal. Knowing
this, I open my heart to the timeless comforts which Spirit provides. I take comfort in the moistening rain, in the scent of flowers, in the tall oak offering me its shade. Even when deeply

troubled, I seek to find Spirit in the midst of my suffering. I soften my heart to the gentle touch of comfort. I allow Spirit to touch my grief.

We are nature.

We are nature seeing nature.

The red-winged blackbird flies in us.

SUSAN GRIFFIN

✑

I LEARN FROM THE EARTH AND ACCEPT ITS WISDOM

The natural world is my mentor and wise companion. I bless the natural world and I allow the natural world to guide me. I allow the rain to teach me its lessons of freshness and renewal. I allow my spirit to be washed clean of any lingering doubts, angers, and anxieties. Washed by the love of Spirit, I am eager and open to undertake new growth. Quenched by divine love, I blossom ever more freely and more fully. Like the rain, I allow myself seasons. I accept loss. I accept change. I expect growth. Like the rain, I am a passing blessing on this earth. I ask that I, too, be a refreshing gift for those who encounter me, that I bless them with tenderness and leave them more refreshed.

Transitions

Prayers and Declarations
for a Changing Life

In loving memoriam

Shari Lewis

I wish to acknowledge two gentlemen
whose artfulness shaped this book:

TIM WHEATER, *composer*

JEREMY TARCHER, *collaborator*

And two gentlewomen:

EMMA LIVELY, *musician*

DORI VINELLA, *muse*

INTRODUCTION

The window of my writing room looks north to Taos Mountain. For me, that mountain is my great teacher. At one moment it looms dark purple against the horizon. Moments later, it is lit by gold. Its folds are crimson and bronze, a transition that happened while I was writing, my attention absorbed by the page.

"Everything changes, is always changing," the mountain reminds me. And yet, it reminds me, too, "There is a bedrock, a level of spiritual reality, that remains always the same."

This book concerns change: the difficulty of change, the possibility of change. It also, at ground level, concerns the acceptance of change. So often we try to live through our changes without experiencing them. When life is difficult, we tune out, focused on the future. "I will be happy," we say, "when this happens" or "when that happens." Or else we say, "I will be happy when this is over." Or, "When that begins."

Focused on life as we yearn for it, we neglect to live the life that we have. "This shouldn't be happening," we tell ourselves in difficult seasons. Meaning, "Once this is over, I'll get on with my life."

Craving the comfort of desired events and outcomes, we ignore the uncomfortable but exhilarating gifts of living life as a continually unfolding process in which all moments are valuable. Absorbed in our "inner movie," we miss the many minute transformations that enrich and ennoble our lives.

In meditation, whether it is three pages of longhand morning writing or twenty minutes of sitting observing our breath, we learn to see the flow of thoughts and perceptions which accompany our lives like a soundtrack. We learn to note and notice our rapidly shifting moods to see that we are the someone who stands somehow apart from those moods, experiencing them like clouds on the face of the mountain. This is the gift of detachment. The prayers in these pages aim at conveying such a gift.

It is usually the emotional burden of a difficult circumstance that causes us to move through it numbly, cut off from our spiritual resources. A sudden illness, the death of a spouse, the unexpected loss of a treasured job, a cherished friend's moving away—any of these may be sufficient to disconnect us from our ongoing sense of the fruitfulness and purpose of life.

"What does it all mean, anyhow?" we may conclude at such

moments. Our shadowed hearts are cut off from the sunlight of the spirit. When we enter such a darkened place it is hard to believe that God, or goodness, can accompany us there.

This book is intended as a conscious companion for difficult times. The prayers directly address many of the difficult transitions that we as humans undergo. This book, however, is intended as something more than a companion. It is also planned as a model for you to work from. The quotes are carefully selected and provocative. I have written my prayers inspired by them and you can as well. The writing of positive, affirmative prayers is a deeply healing spiritual antidote to the pain of anguished moments. Let me give you an example.

The poet Kabir writes, "Wherever you are is the entry point," and that is how to work with writing a prayer. You might write like this:

"Wherever you are is the entry point"

❧ "I stand at the doorway. I am entering the door to my new life. That life is lit by friendship, graced by music, freshly painted because color speaks to my heart . . ."

Taking the same quote, you might equally well write like this:

❧ "I pause as I enter the gate of a new relationship. I take stock of who I am and what I am as myself alone. I appreciate my humor and autonomy, my intellectual curiosity and my creative daring. These I resolve to keep with me. I will retain and cherish my 'I' within our 'We.'"

Equally, you might write:

   ∝ "I am at the threshold of a new business life. I am strong and creative as I step toward my new opportunity. The very gifts that have served me in the past, serve me now. I walk ahead with confidence and conviction in my own competence."

Use this book as a companion in challenging times and as a catalyst to write prayers of your own. It is my experience in many years as an artist and teacher that writing "rights" things. As we move our hand across the canvas of our lives, we paint more vividly the brush-strokes of our experience. Writing is transformative, alchemical, empowering and enlightening. Our transitions become more consciously wrought. As we choose to enter into and cooperate with a difficult passage, we light that passage with the lamp of our personal compassion. By choosing not to abandon ourselves during trying times, we discover the constancy of the Universe loving through us despite all harrowing appearances. When we write the word "I" and claim our experience, we enter the "eye" of the storm, allowing ourselves a steadiness and spiritual constancy even in the midst of strife. It is my hope that this book will be for you both a harbor and a boat.

However confused
the scene of our life appears,
however torn we may be
who now do face that scene,
it can be faced,
and we can go on to be whole.

Muriel Rukeyser

❧

Spirit understands adversity as opportunity. Spirit is able to work for the good in all things. As I encounter difficult transitions in which I doubt the good which is unfolding, I remind myself there is a higher plan in motion with which I can consciously cooperate. As I face my resistance to change, as I choose to align myself with events as they are unfolding, I find in my acceptance a sense of tranquility, a promise of safety. Change embraces me as I myself embrace change.

❧ Today, I surrender my resistance to my hidden yet greater good. I cast my faith forward as a light on my path. I choose to believe in the good which comes toward me. I release my fear.

Every moment
of one's existence
one is growing into more
or retreating into less.
One is always living
a little more
or dying a little bit.

NORMAN MAILER

᯽

All change can be expansive in potential. The choice is ours. As I open my heart to accept change, my heart softens and grows larger. Every experience carries the seed of transformation. Every event can bring blossoming and wealth. My personal will can resist change or embrace it. The choice is mine and determines the life I will have.

᯽ Today, I choose to embrace change. I open my heart to its hidden but abundant blessings.

The primary and most beautiful
of Nature's qualities is motion.

Marquis de Sade

☙

The natural world teaches us the power of change. As seasons shift, I see the purpose and beauty of life's cyclicality. I see the promise of spring, the ripening of summer, the bounty of harvest and the mysterious containment of winter. All seasons work for the good. So it is, too, with the changing cycles of my life. As I surrender to the wisdom of a higher plan, I discover in all circumstances the opportunity for growth and expansion. There is no season in my life that is without worth. There is no season in my life that does not unfold my highest good. Challenged by difficult times, I consciously choose to affirm the goodness of life's timing.

☙ Today, I commit myself to actively seeking the benefit hidden in adversity, the wisdom inherent in all timing.

Wisdom lies
neither in fixity
nor in change,
but in the dialectic
between the two.

Octavio Paz

☙

Curiosity is the right companion of change. It is an attitude that we must elect to hold. As I embrace an attitude of curiosity and wonder, change brings me growth and renewal. It is the key of curiosity which opens the gate to my greater unfolding. As I open my mind and heart, subtle blessings are revealed to me. Life gains new and unexpected graces, colors, textures, and benefits. Curiosity empowers me to explore new dimensions. Curiosity brings me optimism and hope during difficult times.

☙ Today, I embrace my curious nature. I allow curiosity to lead me forward in positive ways through adversity and hardship. My curiosity seeks and discovers buried gifts in all experience.

Today the world changes
so quickly
that in growing up
we take leave
not just of youth
but of the world
we were young in . . .
Fear and resentment
of what is new
is really a lament
for the memories of our childhood.

SIR PETER MEDAWAR

᪥

Resistance solidifies grief. We can allow our griefs to dissolve through releasing them to the healing rain of tears. As we weep with loss, our spiritual landscape is made anew. All change carries gain as well as loss. As I release situations which have troubled me, I release, too, my identity as troubled. This shift brings with it intense emotion. Grief is the natural and healing companion of loss. Embraced and surrendered to, grief creates transformation.

Today, I do not deny my feelings of loss. I allow myself to move through them to new growth.

☙

All of life is interconnected and ongoing. There is no death to the spirit of those I love. As I mourn the physical passing of my beloveds, I open to meet them anew in an ongoing spiritual connection. Subtle but resilient, our relationship goes forward. As I open my heart to continued connection, I encounter the spark of intuition, the lamp of guidance which signals the shared ongoing path. Those who leave me do so only in body. The physical vehicle falls away but the beloved spirit continues to live and even to prosper. Ours is a journey of shared hearts. Death is a passageway, not an ending. As I open my heart to continued connection, my beloveds are carried forward by my love.

⁊ Today, I am brave enough to open to continued connection. I am alert to small signs and signals which speak to me of my beloveds' ongoing presence.

The Lord continually creates,

sustains,

and absorbs all.

He performs all tasks.

SWAMI MUKTANANDA

᠙

Spirit is all-pervasive. Absolutely nothing exists beyond its healing reach. As I move forward through difficult change, Spirit goes before me, preparing a path for me to follow. In Spirit's hands, all change is beneficial. All change works toward the good. There is no problem too small or too large for Spirit to heal and transform. Every detail of my life is relevant to Spirit. There is nothing that I face that I must face alone. In all times of difficulty and discomfort, I turn to Spirit for aid and sustenance. Spirit nurtures me in all circumstances, supports me at every turn.

᠙ Today, I open my heart to accept the help which I am given in all things, both large and small. Today I acknowledge and salute the God force acting in all my affairs.

Friendship is one of the most
tangible things
in a world which offers
fewer and fewer supports.

KENNETH BRANAGH

ॐ

My human loves are cherished companions. I treasure the times we spend together. I salute the importance of our connection, yet I recognize that there are times of appropriate distance. Such transits require an adjustment in attitude. Our hearts must expand rather than contract from loss. In times of separation, I affirm that our connection remains intact through Spirit. Spirit leads our loving hearts and Spirit knows no distance or separation. In Spirit, all things are near, all times are one eternal moment. Taking my lesson from this great teaching, I celebrate connection and continuity in the face of apparent abandonment and loss.

ॐ Today, I acknowledge that all things are one through Spirit. I affirm the presence in the present moment of those who have moved beyond my reach.

Every incident is nourishing,
every circumstance is nourishing,
every word is nourishing,
every sound is nourishing,
because the same love
is in everything and in everyone.

SWAMI CHIDVILASANANDA

Nourishment is spiritual. It is always available to us. The power that we seek is spiritual as well as temporal. In the face of waning health of the body, I affirm a growing health in spirit. Spirit is victorious over illness and even death. Spirit lives on undaunted by physical decline. My spirit is strong and courageous. My spirit is larger than adverse circumstances. I expand into spiritual realms seeking a higher and longer view of current events. As I view the overriding good that works through all and in all, I am able to embrace my destiny and claim the good which it contains.

Today, I claim my spiritual health. I bless and celebrate perfect life within me. I acknowledge that I am a child of the Divine and that my divinity is untouched by adverse conditions. My spirit is triumphant, nourished by God.

This world is nothing but a school of love;
our relationships with our
husband or wife,
with our children and parents,
with our friends and relatives
are the university in which we are meant
to learn what love and devotion
truly are.

SWAMI MUKTANANDA

❧

All of earth is my home. I am nurtured in every place, in every situation. As I leave behind that which is familiar, I find new places where I also find love. Bearing goodwill I find goodwill. I encounter harmony and openness in those I meet. I am embraced. My spirit finds shelter. In my new home, new friends welcome me, making a valued place for me in their lives. I am not alone. Friendships find me.

❧ Today, I embrace the new. I allow my heart to find joy and connection with new companions. I make my heart the hearth at which I warm my spirit. I am at home in every place.

Surely the Holy One is not deaf.
He hears the delicate anklets that ring
on the feet of
an insect as it walks.

KABIR

☙

Divine wisdom underlies all events. No change is without the possibility of benefit. No transition, however harrowing and difficult, fails to bring good. Despite appearances to the contrary, all events unfold according to a higher harmony. I attune myself to this unfolding. I release my doubts, fears and misgivings to a higher hand. By asking Spirit to comfort me, I am cradled in my human frailty yet strengthened in my spiritual connection. I turn to Spirit in all circumstances. I open to the higher good that unfolds through my compliance.

☙ Today, I acknowledge the presence of Spirit in all circumstances. I attune myself to the higher plan that works through me and for me. I expect help and accept it. Divine consciousness is attuned to my needs. I am not unheard.

All the creatures of this cosmos
are sustained by love,
and in the end they merge into
the same cosmic Being.
That is why it is essential to love.

Swami Muktananda

In the divine plan I am partnered by nature—the crimson flash of a cardinal on the wing, the Persian's inscrutable gaze, the silken coat of the cocker spaniel curled by my feet—these are animal companions whom I hold dear. My teachers as well as my friends, my animal companions instruct me to live with devotion and harmony, forgiving slights and inattentions, loving with a sweet and attentive heart. Briefer lived than I, my animal companions teach the joy of living fully, in every moment. As they pass from my realm, I thank them for their selfless love, for the many merry moments that we shared. Bearing their memory in my heart, I am a better companion to all of life.

Today, I salute my animal friends. I celebrate their passage through my life. I allow them to accompany me and also to guide me. I accept their devotion and offer my devoted love in return.

Be a lamp, or a lifeboat, or a ladder.
Help someone's soul heal.
Walk out of your house like a shepherd.

RUMI

☙

Love requires generosity. Love requires daring and expansion. Above all, love requires a dance of differing distances. There is both the pas de deux and the time for solo flight. The dance of love contains both turns. While cherishing our shared time together, I freely release my beloveds to pursue a separate path if that is their destiny. Love connects despite distance. I hold my beloveds tenderly in my heart, trusting that the distance that separates us also brings us together, gifting us with a stronger appreciation of our unique bond. Freedom is a requirement of real love. I honor my beloveds with the gift of freedom.

☙ Today, I open my hand. I release my loved ones to their separate and unique destinies. I cherish them tenderly within my heart while flinging aside the ropes of control that might bind them. I love with an open hand and a resilient heart.

It isn't for the moment
you are struck that you need courage,
but for the long uphill climb
back to sanity
and faith and security.

☙

I nurture a faithful heart. When difficulties, sorrows, and trials beset me, I consciously choose faith in the face of despair. Like the mountain climber who reaches the summit a step at a time, I hold an ideal in my heart. Despite the temptation to bitterness, despite the seduction of rage, I choose a path of temperate endurance, grounding my daily life in the small joys yet available to me. Learning from the natural world, I harbor the seeds of hope against the long winter. I count the small stirrings of beauty and delight still present in a barren time. My heart is a seasoned traveler. Moving through hostile and unfamiliar terrain it remains alert to encounter unexpected beauty blossoming despite the odds. In the arms of adversity, I yet find the comfort of tenderness to myself and others. I refuse to harbor a hardened heart. Decisively and deliberately, I expand rather than contract.

❧ Today, I choose the softening grace of forgiveness. I allow the sunlight of the spirit to reach my shadowed heart.

Kabir says this: just throw away all thoughts of imaginary things,
and stand firm in that which you are.

KABIR

☙

The human heart craves certainty yet life is sometimes uncertain. In times of ambiguity, doubt and apprehension, I claim
the certain safety of my spiritual connection. Reminding myself
that even in the face of difficult change, my grounding in Spirit
remains secure, I find ground on which to stand. Spirit connects
me to all things. It is timeless and serene. Spirit is the bedrock beneath all experience. When I am threatened and adrift, I remind
myself Spirit is an inner fortress, constant and secure.

☙ Today, I embrace Spirit as the rock of my existence. Spirit
gives my soul an earthly home.

All who joy would win
Must share it——Happiness was born
a twin.

<small>LORD BYRON</small>

⌘

S ometimes we are less a person than a place for those we love. Our hearts are the hearth sought by the lonely. I offer those I love the steadiness of my companionship when times grow difficult and dark. Recognizing that my familiar presence offers comfort and dignity to those I cherish, I stand my ground, rooted in the love between us. As my beloveds undergo difficult passages, I walk beside them. I offer compassion, humor, honor for their strength. I am a loving witness. I am steadfast, loyal and strong for those I love.

⌘ Today, I celebrate my role as companion to those I love. I offer witness and good cheer. I light the steady lamp of compassionate attention. My heart is a lantern guide for those I love.

When one man dies,
one chapter is not torn out of the book,
but translated into a better language.

<small>JOHN DONNE</small>

☙

The soul is a traveler through the realm of matter. Our bodies are beloved vehicles housing our souls. The soul is eternal and moves on when it is finished here. The death we see as final is just a door. Faced with the death of one I love, I offer my loving witness of their passage. Grounded in the spiritual truth that life endures, I offer comfort and companionship as my beloved faces the great unknown. Rather than surrender to my own feelings of loss and bereavement, I assure my beloved of love's continuity. Our physical parting does not sever our spiritual ties. Love is the affirmation of life in the face of death. Love is life expanding, living on ever after.

☙ Today, I choose to affirm the great mystery of life eternal, to focus on the Spirit within the body of my beloved. That Spirit lives on.

Suppose you scrub your ethical skin

until it shines,

but inside there is no music,

then what?

KABIR

☙

Work is a part of my identity but it is not my essence. I have a job I may value, yet I am worthy and interesting without my work. The work of the soul transcends our work in the world. I am a soul engaged on a personal journey. I am a traveler whose unique destination can be reached by many routes. Often apparent detours and reversals bring me to new and important vistas, welcome if unexpected growth. While I value my identity as a worker, I affirm the separate and valued identity of the "I" that does the work. Personal and transcendent, "I" am more than any job I undertake. No one job holds my entire destiny.

☙ Today, I affirm my personal value. I see myself as larger than my job. I recognize my inner dignity separate from my worldly role. I allow my soul to shine, my heart to sing.

People seldom see the halting
and painful steps
by which the most
insignificant success is achieved.

ANNE SULLIVAN

CR

The best solutions rarely come to pass swiftly. Time as well as distance may be necessary to the proper unfolding of events. Choosing to honor the longer view, I surrender my sense of urgency and frustration. I allow life to unfurl as a gentle wave. I do not push for instant satisfaction. Mine is a patient heart. Faced with delays and apparent reversals, I remind myself that my greater good often comes from adversity. Choosing to honor the tidal nature of life, I do not push for artificial solutions born of haste and indiscretion. I allow the universe to unfold with divine timing. I attune myself to the tempo of my highest good.

CR Today, I embrace God's timing as my own. Today I place my faith in the divine wisdom that unfolds the seasons each at its proper time. I am a verdant field in the care of universal forces. I allow myself to be nurtured by Divine providence at the proper tempo for my perfect blossoming.

Every instant that the sun is risen,
if I stand in the temple, or on a balcony,
in the hot fields, or in a walled garden,
my own Lord is making love with me.

KABIR

☙

Birth brings me rebirth. My heart expands to encompass new life and new responsibilities. The love of Spirit loves through me, funding me with an abundant flow of gentle affection. I greet the souls that come into my care with tenderness and a sense of adventure. Ours is a shared journey. We are pilgrims traveling together to larger realms. The souls who are my intimates bear gifts for me by their presence. I, too, bear gifts for those I love.

☙ Today, my heart prepares a place for new arrivals. Grounded in Spirit, I am strong, steady and hospitable. A child at heart, I am the welcoming elder to the children that I meet.

It's not the answer that enlightens,
but the question.

EUGENE IONESCO

⌘

Problems bear the seeds of their solutions. Beset by worry or anxiety, unable to clearly see my way, I remind myself my soul is connected to all wisdom. I will be led because I am led firmly and certainly whenever I turn within for guidance. In times of adversity, my store of my own inner wisdom may be greater than I know. At such times, I continue to ask for guidance while listening both within and without for the many small signals which help me to find my way. The guidance of Spirit is always available to me if I quiet my anxiety and listen deeply. Answers come to me from many sources. Solutions emerge where questions are posed.

⌘ Today, with humility and openness I ask for spiritual intervention in my earthly affairs. I ask for help, and, in the asking, it appears.

⚬

Transition creates vulnerability. The safety of the old life has been set aside. The safety of the new life is not yet in place. The passage between the two feels perilous and threatening. Our feet move unsteadily on the rope bridge slung across the jungle chasm and yet, these feelings are illusion. I am safe and secure at all times, in all situations, however unsettling. I claim spiritual safety as the bedrock of my security. My faith is the mountain. Events are the clouds that hide its face. While it may feel at times that events have overwhelmed me, I remind myself that these are passing shadows. My faith endures. My heart, though vulnerable, is protected. The universe intends me good. Choosing to believe that, I find good in adversity. Elected optimism, while difficult to maintain, is spiritually pragmatic. In opening our hearts to the possibility of good within difficulty, we seize the key of curiosity that allows us to open new doors.

Today, I comfort my threatened heart. I affirm my safety in times of change. I accept the comfort of spiritual sunlight. I am warmed by the truth that I am loved and protected even in the midst of chaotic change. Despite my shock, I survey my new spiritual surroundings with a sense of possibility.

Surviving meant
being born
over and over.
Erica Jong

⁂

All beginning is an ending. I both celebrate and grieve. As I choose to start anew in a job, a relationship, a home, I choose to believe in my own resilience. I choose to trust the generosity of life. Calling upon Spirit to supply me, I encounter fulfillment of my wishes, needs and wants. Spirit has abundant supply for my heart's desires. It is the pleasure of Spirit to give. It is my gift back to Spirit to accept. In an antique shop, I find a crystal globe, an antique map that speaks to me of a world lit only by firelight. On a beach, I find the fragile shell washed to me from warmer climes. The falling leaf, vivid and transitory, reminds me of life's cyclicality. A neighbor's wriggling puppy licks my hand. I accept the generosity of Spirit. I allow my life to be made anew.

Today, I embrace the beginning of a better life. I release my grip on the past and open my hand to receive the new. I accept the seeds of the future.

Be strong then,
and enter into your own body;
there you have a solid place for your feet.

KABIR

☙

Our consciousness is independent of our many roles. We define ourselves through work, friendship, family and relationship. When any of these alter we feel cut adrift. "Who am I," I ask, "without . . . ?" Who I am is a child of the entire Universe. My soul has an identity independent of others. My soul has a place that cannot be shaken by external events. Rooted in Spirit, my soul is ever-cherished, ever known and beloved.

☙ Today, I choose Spirit as the source of my identity. I embrace self-love and self-definition. I am worthy and cherished in changing times.

If you want the truth,
I'll tell you the truth:
Listen to the secret sound, the real sound,
which is inside you.

KABIR

❧

The body is a great teacher. Spirit and body work as a team. In times of bodily illness, I seek spiritual health. I turn within to Spirit, tapping the deep resources of Universal well-being. As I focus on spiritual healing, I experience an undercurrent of wellness that underlies my current experience. As a Spirit, I am healthy. I am vibrant and eternal. Focused on this reality, I gain strength. I gain clarity and resilience. My spiritual energies fund my physical self with support and sustenance.

❧ Today, I focus on the reality that Spirit infuses all of matter and that Spirit is perfect and eternal. I claim the perfect health that is mine as Spirit. I feel myself vibrant and whole.

Our Friendship is made
of being awake.

RUMI

℘

Attention is the gift of solitude. Thrown back on my own resources, deprived of the company of those I love, I learn to cherish my own companionship. As I discover my independence, I also discover my interdependence. I see the gentle and intricate dance of our connection. I perceive the steps I know and the steps I would like to learn. Making good use of my solitude for reflection, I connect deeply to myself, thereby strengthening my capacity to connect with others. I also learn with clarity what it is I love and miss in my companions. Separation teaches both autonomy and connection.

℘ Today, I focus on my relationship to myself. I reach within and make contact with my own spiritual resources. I experience the inner wealth that is mine to share. I connect deeply with myself in preparation for joining with others.

Such is the state of life,
that none are happy but by the
anticipation of change:
the change itself is nothing;
when we have made it, the next wish is
to change again.
The world is not yet exhausted;
let me see something tomorrow
which I never saw before.

SAMUEL JOHNSON

CS

Sometimes it is the seasons in life which are without drama that are the most challenging. As life unfolds smoothly but without heightened adrenaline, we experience a sense both of tranquility and loss. We miss a sense of drama that allows us to define ourselves in terms of our reactions to outer events. In the absence of dramatic events, we are asked to turn within and define ourselves. This can feel frightening, as if we are in an unfamiliar world without landmarks. Who are we in the absence of heightened stress? In peaceful moments, what do we truly desire?

The deeper streams of my temperament run strong but quiet. To hear them, I must listen.

❧ Today, I turn my attention to deep inner listening. I attune my spiritual hearing to finer and finer levels as I listen for the subtle ongoing guidance that comes to me in quiet times.

The meeting of two personalities
is like the contact of
two chemical substances:
if there is any reaction, both
are transformed.

C. G. JUNG

CS

Connections are alchemical. Friendships are not static. They are living entities that grow and change. Sometimes my friendships become strained, undergoing mysterious seasons of estrangement. I allow my friendships to alter and grow. I allow them to fall fallow and rest quietly until the season comes for them to bloom again. I do not demand my friendships always be easy. I grant to my friends the freedom to grow, to change, and to challenge me by their altered behaviors and views. I release my friends to their personal trails and timing. I do not take personally their occasional needs for distance and self-containment. My friendships are organic and evolutionary. My friendships are catalytic and transformative. Our intersections spark new growth.

∞ Today, I am flexible and evolutionary. I am a meadow with varied seasons and wealth in each one. I am blessed with abundance and I am abundant in the blessings that I offer to others. The right to change is a blessing that I offer to my friends. We are miners striking new ore at every depth.

The changes in our life
must come from the impossibility
to live otherwise
than according to the demands
of our conscience.

LEO TOLSTOY

⌘

Each of us has an inner compass. Its voice calls us to our highest good. Sometimes it requires that we alter a long-standing but stifling situation. It is difficult to face the severing or alteration of a relationship even when we know such change is for the highest good. Faced with a divorce or separation, faced with the need to terminate a long-standing friendship, I must remind myself that sometimes the most loving involvement is a non-involvement. It is tempting, always, to try to go back, to hold onto what once was rather than face what that relationship has now become. I resolve with a loving heart to accept appropriate endings. I do not grasp at straws when the reality is difficult but clear. Instead, I release the past, bless it and turn with resolution to the future. I listen to the dictates of my conscience, knowing that its voice calls me home.

೭ Today, I place my humbled heart in universal care, asking for healing and direction.

Let the great world spin
for ever down
the ringing grooves of change.

Lord Tennyson

❦

The world is a forest of verdant possibility. No one person controls my happiness. No one person is the source of my joy. I am rooted in universal flow. My needs for love and affection are met by many sources. I am blessed by the ability to receive love through many channels. I open my heart to the love that is offered to me by multiple sources. My heart is a mountain meadow fed by many streams.

❦ Today, I practice receptivity to loving forces. At any moment, a divinely inspired intersection may occur. I accept the good which flows to me from many sides.

Nothing that grieves us
can be called little:
by the eternal laws of proportion
a child's loss of a doll
and a king's loss of a crown are
events of the same size.

MARK TWAIN

All risk risks rejection. The sting of criticism can create a spiral of shame. Bitten by shame, it is easy to become embittered, to shrink back from life and slide toward despair. I do not allow myself this dangerous luxury. Faced with hostility I turn within for spiritual comfort, reminding myself I am a child of the Universe, worthy of love, care and respect. Aware of my vulnerability, I treat myself gently with the same care I would extend to an injured friend. My dignity is grounded in my spiritual identity. I hold my worth in the face of hostility. I am unshaken by the sting of personal assault. I allow my heart to be a fortress. My spirit is like the face of a mountain proud and bright in the sun.

Today, I stand firm in my own worthiness. My dignity is solid and enduring. My faith is the rock on which I build my life. I dare to risk and I risk my daring. I am large enough to survive my losses and enjoy my gains.

Though lovers be lost love shall not;
And death shall have no dominion.

DYLAN THOMAS

❧

We rely on those we love to be our sounding boards. Their perceptions and opinions are part of what we love. When we lose our loved ones, we do not lose their interactions with us. Instead, we are asked to listen more acutely for the guidance that they offer. This guidance may come to us as intuition. It may come to us as memory. It may come to us as friends and strangers speaking to us in the tone of our lost love. As we open our hearts to continued relationship with those who have passed on, we find ourselves helped at many turns, protected in many ways. Our loved ones continue to love us as we do them. As we open our hearts and our minds to their continued love, we are reminded by a sense of their presence.

❧ Today, I allow myself to be aided and guided by those who have gone before. Just as the mighty tree springs from the tiny seed, my full flowering is rooted in all that have gone before me. I celebrate the continuity of life. I am part of a larger whole and it is a part of me.

Stop the words now.
Open the window in the center
of your chest,
and let the spirits fly in and out.

RUMI

In our lives, we are many sizes, experiencing ourselves as both large and small. Often a change for the better can cause us to actually feel worse. We doubt our worthiness of the good that has come our way. We temporarily feel small, out of our depth, off-center. Our dreams are coming true and we do not feel large enough to inhabit them. We shrink back in the face of the life we have created. In such times of self-diminishment, I remind myself: I am the flower of God. My life blossoms through God. The good which comes to me is God's business, not my own. When I allow my life to open and bloom, I am allowing God to find expression in the world.

Today, I surrender my resistance to being large. I allow God to choose my size for me.

True friendship is a plant
of slow growth,
and must undergo and withstand
the shocks of adversity
before it is entitled to the appellation.

GEORGE WASHINGTON

CR

Friendships require honesty and honesty requires courage. In all friendships there are moments when we must choose to be courageous. Our friendships have become root-bound and so must be repotted, transplanted and transformed into a larger and healthier vessel. This transition requires us to speak the difficult truth. Speaking our hearts' truth, while not always easy, yields us the bedrock on which the friendship stands firm. As I choose to speak with integrity and openness, I commit more deeply both to myself and to others. As I learn to trust the safety of open communication, I find that I open like a plant responding to the sun. Honesty is healing and nutritious to my heart and its friendships.

❧ Today, I blossom in honesty and openness. Today, I allow the nutrition of honest communication to foster my relationships to greater health.

The sun sets and the moon sets,
but they're not gone. Death is
a coming together.

RUMI

❧

Death is both dramatic and subtle. Over time, the parting of a loved one becomes less harsh as slowly and gently a continued bond is revealed. As I open my heart to the promptings and guidance of those I love who have passed from the physical sphere, I am alert to the contact which comes to me in many forms—as memory, as intuition and coincidence. Rather than bitterly close my heart, I allow myself to maintain a gentle but alert attention to the touch of Spirit. I remind myself that life begets life and that those I love live on in my loving memory of them. I also allow for the possibility that my memory lives on in them, triggering their concerned contact in subtle forms.

❧ Today, I deliberately practice open-mindedness. I cultivate a willingness to experience subtle realms.

Fortunately psychoanalysis
is not the only way
to resolve inner conflicts.
Life itself still remains a very
effective therapist.

KAREN HORNEY

In daily life there is an inner transition I can consciously practice. This is the transition from fear to faith. Faced with ambiguity and uncertainty, I can choose to believe things will work
out for the best. The lost job will yield me a new and better one.
The difficult friendship set aside yields room for new friends to
enter. The novel direction taken by my current thought will prove
fruitful, not merely eccentric. All is working toward the good.
Rather than indulge in worry and second-guessing, I can elect to
believe there is wisdom in the unfolding of events exactly as they
are. For many, the decision to switch from fear to faith is a decision to switch from pessimism to optimism. As we choose to be
open-minded and optimistic about our lives, we are graced with

an alert attention to our own unfolding good. I am a witness to my own miraculous growth.

❧ Today, I choose conscious optimism. My life is God's field planted with the seeds of my future blossoming.

To keep a lamp burning
we have to keep
putting oil in it.

<small>MOTHER TERESA</small>

❧

Communication is often difficult. Friendships may become clouded by unspoken and unshared feelings. In times when my friendships are shadowed by such secrecy, I remind myself that I can hold a bright lamp in my heart, waiting for the right time to gently clear the air. Listening with an inner ear for the proper moment to present itself, I resolve to bravely but softly share my feelings, thoughts and insights. Rather than harbor anger or resentment when communication is stifled, I pray for the well-being of my estranged friend, communicating on a spiritual level my continued commitment to our bond.

❧ Today, I renew my inner commitment to honesty. Today, I listen for right timing for when to speak my heart. Alert and willing to follow inner guidance, I choose my moment and my words with healing grace.

Everything is so dangerous
that nothing
is really very frightening.

GERTRUDE STEIN

☙

As we travel, we change cultures and consciousness. Our sense of self may be both heightened and shaky. Traveling, I am opened to new outer vistas and new inner perspectives. I am taught to view life from a higher angle, to gain a sense of my placement against a broader canvas. We are travelers at all times, although we seldom view life as the journey that it is. Traveling, I gain a sense of my personal trajectory. I take stock, measuring my progress toward perceived goals. Freed from the ordinary structure of my life, I am freed, too, to evaluate that life, to ascertain whether its outer form matches my inner needs. Life can be led in myriad ways. Viewing my many options, I select my own favored path.

☙ Today, I view myself as a pilgrim. I take stock of the distances I have traveled. I take time to map the route I now choose.

❧

Illness shocks us body and soul. Its suffering forces us into new territory. While we are often unable to find a cause for our disease, we are often moved to greater spiritual opening. As well as the bitter fruits of pain and trauma, we harvest the more subtle gifts of openness and acceptance. As we face the challenge of an illness striking unfairly and without warning, we also inventory the richness of the life that it interrupts. We may discover we have lived fully, lovingly and well. We may realize the depth of the bonds with those we cherish. Sudden and catastrophic illness is a spiritual trapdoor that plummets us into the net of the Universe. In our free fall, we often discover surprising faith and acceptance. We are ambushed into our spiritual health.

Today, I find health in my illness. Today, I find well-being at the core of my dis-ease. I accept the condition unexpectedly thrust upon me. With this new landmark, I find my spiritual bearings and greater growth.

The call of death is a call of love.
Death can be sweet if we answer it
in the affirmative,
if we accept it as one of the great eternal
forms of life and transformation.

There are no compassionate words strong enough to hold our suffering hearts in the face of death. It is the loving intention beneath the words, running through them, that forms the net for our falling hearts. Even as we tumble to the depths of despair, we are caught in the net of compassion. There are those who love us as we have loved. There are those who have suffered loss as we do. Every love is unique and individual. Every loss is personal and particular. Yet the great web of life embraces one and all. Our suffering is a known suffering. Our healing is an eventuality toward which all the Universe tends. As we enter the portals of grief, we are met by the understanding of the ages. Birth, love, and death are landmarks of the human condition. As I open my heart to accept the reality of a beloved's passing, I open my heart to my own humanity. Rather than isolate myself, feeling somehow special in my grief, I choose to see that my sorrow is the sorrow of the ages—poignant, personal and particular, yet universal in nature.

❧ Today, I accept my tears of grief as the life-giving rain that fosters new growth. Even in the face of death itself, I feel the resiliency of life moving me inexorably onward to greater good.

When the mind becomes quiet,
you feel nourished.

SWAMI CHIDVILASANANDA

❧

Some seasons are less colorful than others. Temperate, even boring, such times require we creatively seek our own diversions. The soul has many weathers. In times of calm, I remind myself that growth occurs slowly and steadily. When I am tempted to artificially stir up drama in my environment, I remind myself that drama often diverts deeper and more substantial growth. My heart is a serene woodland lake. The winds of change ripple it lightly.

❧ Today, I allow subtlety in my own unfolding. I value serenity. I cherish peace.

Change is not made
without inconvenience.

RICHARD HOOKER

☙

C hange creates friction and friction creates change. As we welcome the new, we must surrender the old. Our developing life requires that we make room for it. As we sort papers, clean drawers and clear closets, we are ordering far more than our physical life. As we create harmony, we attract harmony. Our lives become sweeter, less chaotic, more flowing. Clearing away the physical blocks to a serene environment, I clear away the psychic blocks to personal serenity. Change, however inconvenient, creates convenience and flow.

☙ Today, I am a clear stream flowing softly through green meadows. I make my way swiftly but gently to my goals.

Let that which stood in front go behind,
Let that which was behind advance
to the front.

Walt Whitman

⊂∂

Loss transforms perspective. The pain of loss can be stagger-ing. Struck down by grief and longing, it is difficult to cope and more difficult to imagine life regaining sweetness. In seasons of mourning, care must be taken. We must consciously and cre-atively choose to fill our days with gentle good. This means we must focus our attention on the present moment, scanning its particular delights even if from an emotional distance. The cat in the window. The geranium blooming on a sill. The golden re-triever bounding at its owner's side. Each of these singular sights can touch the frozen heart, gently waking it to new life even amidst pain. In severe seasons of heartache we are asked to pro-tect and care for ourselves like vulnerable children taking a child-like delight in the tiny joys of life.

～ Today, I choose to cherish myself like a beloved child. I treat myself gently and with compassion. Practicing alert attention, I find delight in the small treasures of the day. I allow meaningful moments to assume enhanced perspective. Counting these blessings, I enrich my impoverished heart.

Help your brother's boat across,
and lo! your own has reached the shore.

HINDU PROVERB

◌

The world is an ocean of possibility. Relationships deepen and alter. As we move beyond our accustomed depth, new attitudes and shells are required. It is like learning to swim. The water will support us if we learn to allow it. So, too, in relationships, we must develop the faith necessary to float as well as to strive. Just as a swimmer must learn to trust the waters that hold him, we must learn to trust that the relationship can support the weight of our personality. Rather than constant effort we must relax and allow ourselves to trust the subtle energies of love. All relationships require vulnerability. As I learn to open to this fact, I soften into a flexible strength.

◌ Today, I practice faith in my unfolding relationship. Like an autumn leaf borne on the wind, I allow myself to be carried gently forward.

Change means movement.
Movement means friction.

SAUL ALINSKY

⁓

Physical change invites spiritual change. Our physical bodies are the vehicles that carry us through life. As we alter our physical appearance, our interactions with others are also affected. Time and compassion are required to adjust to shifts in our personal appearance. A gain or loss of weight, a new hairstyle or color, a shift in clothing—any of these may open the door to feelings of vulnerability, even fragility. Conversely, as we strengthen our bodies, we may feel the power of our own magnetism, the energy of our sexuality, the gift of our own attractive nature. I remind myself life is seasonal and that as my appearance alters, I am moving through a shift which I will weather with grace, dignity, even humor. My "changing look" alters my outlook. I accept the expanded vision that comes to me as a gift of my altered self.

⁓ Today, I treat myself with compassion. I embrace my altered persona and I accept the many changes that it brings.

Love doesn't just sit there like a stone,
it has to be made,
like brick; re-made all the time,
made new.

Ursula K. LeGuin

෨

I build my friendships with the conscious architecture of my integrity. My design contains space for change. My friendships are flexible and resilient. I do not demand that my relationships remain static and unvarying. Instead, I allow my bonds to be mutable and varied. At times I am close and at times I am more distant from even my closest friends. Such is the natural tide of relationships. I accept the changing tides of my friendships. I allow flow and mutability. My heart is a spiritual shoreline with intricate tides that I honor and respect.

෨ Today, I respect the changing garden of my life. I focus on those areas that are in blossom and I allow other areas to lie fallow knowing they, too, will blossom in their turn.

Often God shuts a door
in our face,
And then subsequently opens the door
through which we need to go.

CATHERINE MARSHALL

☙

The heart is more daring and resilient than we often imagine. Faced with the grief of a relationship altering, we often feel both unloved and unloving, as if we have exhausted our capacity for love. There is a larger truth. We are immersed in love, a part of love and a portal for love to love through us. Reminding myself I am loved by divine love and able to love through divine love, I allow my heart to soften and dissolve its wounding. I allow my heart to open into compassion. Loving myself through the conscious acceptance of my vulnerability, I embrace my ability to transform and transcend.

☙ Today, I allow the alchemy of divine love to transform a difficult ending into a new beginning. My heart is a phoenix and today I celebrate its flight.

Courage is the price
that life exacts
for granting peace.
AMELIA EARHART

ॐ

Sometimes our lives are torn asunder. The tornado of change comes to us swiftly and seemingly without mercy. What was, is no longer. We are cast adrift. The fabric of our existence is torn end to end. Even in times of such extreme transition, there is an underlying working toward the good. Even in times in which grief blinds us, in which we rage against our fate, there is a tide that can move us toward growth and healing.

ॐ Today, I consciously and deliberately soften my heart against bitterness. I ask the healing grace of universal love to comfort me and draw me to new beginnings. I choose to release from my heart its bitter trauma and its shock. I accept the deeper growth I am offered through my terrible sorrow. I open my heart by asking for universal forces to aid me in my time of need.

There is a Secret One inside us;
the planets in all the galaxies
pass through his hands like beads.
That is a string of beads one should look
at with luminous eyes.

KABIR

❧

We are like jewelers. At the start of any day, we have before us the beautiful beads of differing choices. Choice by choice, moment by moment, I build the necklace of my day, stringing together the choices that form artful living. Will I be quiet today or outgoing, solitary or involved with friends, reflective or expressive? Will I write letters, make phone calls, pay bills, sweep floors or go for a good long walk? Moving through my days with conscious grace, I connect to the web of life. I, too, am a bead in a larger pattern.

❧ Today, I choose to live by conscious design, nurturing myself and others in body, mind and spirit. I ask for and receive guidance in my choices. I cherish the pattern of my life.

We can never go back again,
that much is certain.

DAPHNE duMAURIER

☙

Sometimes people fail us in terrible ways. We are betrayed, abandoned, cast aside. In times of such personal trauma, we must hold to the larger picture. The Universe does not betray us. The Universe does not leave our side. Even in the midst of grievous loss, we are led and comforted. We are cared for and protected. Although I may fail to see it, a higher hand operates in my affairs. I realize that while people may indeed fail me and turn away, there is an underlying goodness to the Universe which brings to me new friends and new situations. These gifts heal and soothe me. I see the merciful hand of providence despite my pain.

☙ Today, I place my trust in universal love. I open my heart to receive care and comfort from unexpected sources. I allow my good to come from many quarters. I surrender my fixed ideas as to what best serves me. I open to the innovative grace of my unfolding life.

One is happy as a result
of one's own efforts, once one
knows the necessary ingredients
of happiness—simple tastes,
a certain degree of courage,
self-denial to a point,
love of work, and above all,
a clear conscience.
Happiness is no vague dream,
of that I now feel certain.

GEORGE SAND

Happiness is a by-product of right living. Right action leads us to right thinking. In some seasons, we are able to act decisively in directions that please us and feel happiness as a result. At other times, life is less linear and more variable. Happiness is more elusive as we experience events and timing beyond our control. Among life's vivid seasons, there are also times of a more muffled love, periods of muted mood and ambivalent, even ambiguous feelings. These are the limbo times, the gray days that fall in between. These are the transitional times when I am not what I was nor am yet what I am becoming. In limbo times, I must live with alert attention to my feelings of vulnerability. I must guard against hasty choices and rushed decisions. In limbo times I must learn to simply be. Soon enough life will move me onward.

☙ Today, I practice the action of loving non-action. I allow my life to alter organically and without unnatural haste. I trust the tempo of my unfolding.

Thinkers, listen, tell me
what you know of that is not
inside the soul?

Kabir

❧

The heart has dreams and hopes it hides from public view. The heart has secret sorrows, private woes. Listening to my heart, I must listen with gentle ears. If I judge too harshly, my heart will not speak of disappointments and their pain will remain. My heart requires my tenderness to speak its secrets. My heart rewards my love by being the true compass by which I may steer my life.

❧ Today, my heart is safe within my keeping. I offer my heart compassionate ears to hear its dreams.

☙

New skills lend sparkle to our lives. Hobbies enrich the soul. The piano learned for joy, the handmade sweater knit for a cherished niece, the newly painted kitchen chair—these actions light our daily lives. A small simple homely poem, a pot of soup, a brightly colored leaf pressed into a book—these are the beautiful stones my home is built upon. I can accomplish some beauty in every day. I can add to my world by my artfulness.

☙ Today, I act in small and concrete ways to bring beauty to my home. I allow the hand of the Great Creator to work through me, bringing grace and order to my surroundings.

It is change,
continuing change,
inevitable change,
that is the dominant factor
in society today.
<small>ISAAC ASIMOV</small>

Sometimes we are faced with events beyond our control. Our friends accept jobs in distant cities. The one we love falls suddenly and irrevocably in love with someone else. Our company downsizes. A fire sweeps our neighborhood and our house is lost in flames. Faced with such losses, our hearts are seized by fear. We feel swept beyond our depth, adrift in a dangerous sea. The world appears a hostile and forbidding place. We are frightened. At times like these, we draw into ourselves, contracting our hearts self-protectively. It is a natural reflex—and it is counter to our good. In times of adversity, we must expand, not contract. We must open, not close. We must open our hand to receive aid rather than clutch tightly to what we have remaining.

Today, I let go. I release my defenses. Rather than hold myself tightly curled into the fist I use to fight adversity, I open my heart's hand to allow the touch of friendship, the touch of hope. Rather than harden my heart against further blows, I soften it to receive new beginnings.

You must do the thing
you think you cannot do.

ELEANOR ROOSEVELT

❧

Optimism in the face of uncertainty is a difficult art. The terrain of life is varied and mysterious. I cannot always see the path ahead. At times my view is shadowed by doubt, constricted by fear. The open vistas of optimism are closed to me. In such short-sighted times, I must practice the discipline of positive attitudes. I must consciously choose to expect a benevolent future despite my shaken faith. Grounded in the routine of each day's unfolding business, I must act in alignment with my coming good. This means I say "yes" to opportunities for new adventures and acquaintances to enter my life. I say "yes" to unexpected doors opening. Rather than cling to my known life, I allow that life to alter and expand. I choose to take positive risk. I step out in faith despite my misgivings.

❧ Today, I open my mind and heart to the new vistas before me. I embrace change and accept unfolding possibilities. I am a fertile field available for God's planting.

The things that have
come into being
change continually.

Augusto Roa Bastos

☙

As we move to embrace new vistas, we are not asked to abandon those we love. As life leads me forward—to a new job, a new home, a new relationship—I do not need to close my heart to all that has gone before. My heart is a worthy vessel. It carries riches gained from my living adventures. It carries room enough for other riches to be gathered. I move through life like a trader, bringing gifts to those I meet and leaving their sides enriched by the gifts they bear for me. Life is always bountiful, always adventurous, if I will open my heart to the new lands being offered. As a spiritual sailor, I must lift the sail of faith and allow destiny's wind to move me forward.

☙ Today, I welcome the winds of change. Today I cooperate with the new experiences coming to my soul.

There are sounds to seasons.
There are sounds to places,
and there are sounds to every
time in one's life.

ALISON WYRLEY BIRCH

⌘

We often speak of desiring "sound" lives without realizing how telling the phrase is. By focusing on the sound of my life, I can alter and improve my life. What is the tone of my voice? What is the tone of my environment? As I focus on the "pitch" of my life, I can create harmony. My voice, the music I choose, even the tone of my prayers—all these factors contribute to my life's being "sound."

⌘ Today, I live gently and harmoniously. Today, I voice praise, gratitude and healing.

All that is necessary
to make this world a better place
to live is to love—to love as
Christ loved, as Buddha loved.

ISADORA DUNCAN

⁂

We do not interact at random. We are in each other's lives for spiritual reasons. We have "business" with one another. By consciously choosing to focus on why I have met someone, on how I can best serve and expand another, I bring to each encounter a heightened awareness. As I ask to love all and serve all, I bring forward my spiritual gifts and call forward the gifts of others. Grace fills every moment when we are truly present. Sometimes we transit each other's lives like benevolent planets.

⁂ Today, I ask to be a loving and expansive presence for those whom I meet. I offer myself as a loving conduit for the goodness of the Universe to move through me, blessing all I encounter.

Spiritual power can be seen
in a person's reverence
for life—hers and all others,
including animals and nature,
with a recognition of a universal
life force referred to by
many as God.

VIRGINIA SATIR

❧

Unity charges all of life. One energy connects us all, linking us soul to soul and heart to heart. At any time, in any place, I can go within and feel my connection to all of life. As spiritual beings, we are vast and mysterious. The heart is generous and capacious. The heart is far-reaching and all-inclusive. The heart can contain far-flung loves. The heart can love despite geography.

❧ Today, my heart holds all my beloveds close despite the distance between us. Today my heart is full of connections, alive with the knowledge of the tender web which holds us all in its embrace.

The influence of a beautiful,
helpful, hopeful character
is contagious, and may
revolutionize a whole town.

ELEANOR H. PORTER

෫

My heart is a tiny town welcoming those who enter. I can choose to be open or closed to those whom I meet, and so, I choose to be open. My attitude determines the caliber of our interactions. As I consciously choose a welcoming heart, I bring to the world a place where dynamic and healing interactions can occur. I am a single soul, yet that soul is a bright lantern. I become medicine for all I encounter. I, too, am healed by the balm of an open heart. Rather than diminish my importance by saying "I am only one," I choose instead to be a useful instrument in the unfolding of a better world. I consciously align myself with the highest good, asking always to be guided and empowered. In my family, my business and my community I work to make this earth a better place. Mine is a hospitable heart.

Today, I greet life with openness, wonder and curiosity. I offer respectful interest and attention to all. I salute the wisdom, dignity and grace of those whom I encounter.

It is good to have an end
to journey towards;
but it is the journey that matters,
in the end.

URSULA K. LEGUIN

My life is fruitful and abundant. Just as the earth has its cycles and seasons, so, too, our own lives have times of planting, times of growth and times of harvest. So much of my frustration comes from my refusal to accept life's seasons as they come to me. An adolescent child enters a period of rebellion. This is necessary to full maturation. A project at the midpoint is sprawling and unwieldy. This, too, is necessary. A marriage enters a time of solo growth and trajectories as each partner pursues independent interests. However unsettling, this, too, is healthy. Not all seasons lie serene in the sun, yet each has its place. As I ask to be attuned to life's cycles, I feel my anxiety slipping away. I rest in the faith that all is unfolding according to right timing. I am where I should be when I should be. I am alert to the good of every moment.

℘ Today, I accept divine timing. I allow the pacing of the Universe to be my own. I align myself with the tempo of my life precisely as it is unfolding.

If you want the truth,
I will tell you the truth:
Friend, listen: the God whom I love
is inside.

KABIR

❧

One life, one love, one energy runs through all of creation. This Life is Spirit, an inner river that can be tapped into at any time. Knowing this, we are divinely guided at all times. In any place, in any circumstance, the Inner Voice has clarity and direction for me, if I will seek it out. Often it is just an act of focusing that brings the sense of direction more fully into play. When outward events jostle me with their velocity and turbulence, I must actively turn within, seeking higher perceptions.

❧ Today, I release the urgency of outer events. I listen to the inner rhythm of God. I set my pace by divine guidance. The world and its busy agendas do not control my soul. My soul rests in God: good, orderly direction.

374

Life is measured
by the rapidity of change.

GEORGE ELIOT

ॐ

L ife is often turbulent. The rapids and eddies of the day's events may pull at our consciousness like tiny hands. Beneath the turbulence of daily living, there is a longer, slower pulse of perfect timing. It is to that rhythm that I give my soul. I listen beneath the turbulence of daily life. I open myself to the guidance of higher forces. I ask for and receive adjustments in my priorities. I allow myself to find the tempo most attuned to my personal unfolding.

ॐ Today, I act and react with a sense of the larger view, the truer goals. I give myself assurance that God's timing is my own and serves my own best interests.

Most of the change we think
we see in life
Is due to truths being in
and out of favor.

ROBERT FROST

ॐ

We are evolutionary and revolutionary. As we grow and evolve, our inner identities shift. Sometimes outer circumstances move more slowly. Old forms and images mask the emerging truth. When that happens, we are often frustrated, feeling that people do not see us for who we truly are. At such times patience and communication are key. I must give people both the time and the information necessary to know me anew. In my friendships, I must marshall an alert attention, seeing others with a fresh eye as they, too, change and evolve. The truth of who we are and who our friends are must allow for the possibility of continual redefinition. Respect for the changes in myself and others deepens and enriches the garden of friendship.

ᴄꙅ Today, I take the time to get my friends and acquaintances current on the shifts in my inner life. I communicate clearly and openly. I allow time for people to adjust to the ways in which I have changed. I, too, adjust to the change in others.

Whatever you receive,
wherever it comes from,
cherish the desire to give it back
in full measure.

SWAMI CHIDVILASANANDA

ॐ

Sometimes, even in the midst of a busy and crowded life, we are pierced by loneliness. We long to be understood, to feel a sense of deep and enduring companionship. If only, we think, I had someone with whom I could share myself internally, on all levels. If only I had a true companion . . . At these times, we must look to the ways we are always perfectly partnered, carefully and deeply guarded and guided by the Universe itself. The Universe never abandons us. There is always a perfect partnering, a constant and continual reaching out to each of us.

ॐ Today, I remind myself that despite my loneliness I am not alone. I turn my attention to the unique partnering that comes to me from many quarters. I accept the companionship of an interactive Universe. I am with friends.

With an eye made quiet by the power
Of harmony, and the deep power of joy,
We see into the life of things.

WILLIAM WORDSWORTH

CB

Modern life can feel dangerous and unstable. Removed from a sense of natural unfolding, our lives can seem precarious and chaotic. Both business and busy-ness can distract us from realizing the deeper flow. We may feel only the rapids and not the nurturing waters. In times of such stress and anxiety, I seek a foundation firmer than the choppy flow of external events. Like a tree buffeted by the wind, I am yet grounded in the deep soil of my spiritual life. My roots are strong and self-nurturing. They draw to me sustenance and support.

CB Today, I root myself in the earth. I connect to the seasons and cycles of life, the great wheel of nature that sustains us all. I reach beneath my daily life, funding my soul with the grace that underlies all things. I am grounded in life itself.

No trumpets sound
when the important decisions
of our life are made.
Destiny is made known silently.

AGNES DEMILLE

꙳

Life is verdant and generous despite times of drought, doubt and despair. New beginnings are subtle and in my pain and impatience I can often overlook the shoots of fresh growth tenaciously winning through even in difficult times. It takes an alert attention to recognize and appreciate my small gains in seasons of adversity. I choose to consciously focus on the gently growing good. As I choose to see my progress I can offer myself honor for my tenacity, my resilience and my faith.

꙳ Today, I open my eyes to my own gentle progress. I recognize and salute my courage. I applaud my small gains and offer myself compassion for being a work in progress.

We tend to think of the rational
as a higher order,
but it is the emotional
that makes our lives.
One often learns more from
ten days of agony
than from ten years of contentment.

MERLE SHAIN

CS

Sometimes change is sudden and catastrophic. Life as we know it is abruptly overturned. We have an earthquake of the heart so severe that the landscape will never look the same. In times of sudden chaos, the soul finds its ground in the eternal. It turns instinctively toward God, even if it uses other names. An acute listening takes hold as the soul attunes itself to hear more deeply. This deeper listening is an automatic response as natural as breathing.

CS Today, I listen with my deepest heart. I am alert and responsive to guidance in many forms and formats. As I open my attention to a broad range of cues, I find myself guided and guarded. My heart is anchored in spiritual seas. Storms rise and pass yet I survive.

. . . that is what learning is.
You suddenly understand
something you've understood all your life,
but in a new way.

DORIS LESSING

❧

A change in perception can be as radical as turning on the lights in a darkened room. Suddenly we see what we could not see before. Our eyes are opened. Our necessary path becomes clear. Such breakthroughs into clarity can be shocking, even painful. What I now see is an uncomfortable truth. I must change to accommodate my unsparing vision. I must accept what I have long denied. In times of such poignant awakening, I must be patient and gentle with my startled self. Clarity is the bedrock of an honest life. That foundation is what I am building.

❧ Today, I gently and resolutely face difficult truths. I open my eyes to facing that which I have found unfaceable. Remembering that sight brings insight, I invite the sunlight of the spirit to illuminate my life.

ஐ

The world is peopled by travelers each with a journey. As we make our way through our own obstacles, we are often oblivious to those who travel by our side. And yet when we open our hearts to the adventures and adversities of others, our own journey is illumined. Those who travel beside me are my teachers and those I teach in turn.

ஐ Today, I turn my attention to the lives of others. I open to the interactive dance of our intersecting lives. Alert and attentive, I learn from those around me. Empathetic and involved, I teach what I have learned. Ours is a journey of shared hearts. I lift the lantern of camaraderie.

Imagination has always had powers
of resurrection
that no science can match.

INGRID BENGIS

⌘

Much of modern life is stressful and cacophonous. It is both chaotic and disturbing in the frequent turbulence and velocity of change. Maintaining a sense of calm and even flow is an elusive goal that is attained through gently maintaining a spiritual practice amidst the hubbub of our secular lives. Spiritual practice is central to my sense of well-being. Nothing takes precedence over my soul's unfolding. I take the time and make the effort to touch base with myself on a spiritual level throughout the day.

⌘ Today, I take time to practice spiritual deepening. Setting aside a few moments for quiet contemplation, I turn my attention inward to a calm center in my heart. There, in the meadow of stillness, I pause to refresh my spirit.

Man's yesterday may ne'er be like
his morrow;
Nought may endure but Mutability.

❧

E lders walk before us. The young follow behind. Ours is a
caravan of consciousness. The sands of Spirit shift beneath
our feet as we trudge together toward a future we are all of us
making. Ours is an elective and a collective adventure. We add to
the whole by our conscious participatory humanity. Each of us is
important. Each indispensable. As I choose to act and interact,
kindly and generously, my world becomes a kinder and more generous world.

❧ Today, I embrace the longer view. I see my place in the great
scheme of human events.

☙

When we are engaged deeply with others, our changes often come to us as a result of theirs. When a spouse or child sustains a stunning loss, we, too, feel it. When a loved one achieves heady success, their fearful giddy uncertainty, painful insecurity or jubilant grandiosity becomes ours to deal with. Even rooted as we are in our own individuality, nonetheless we live in community and commiseration with those we love. Often our love is a shelter when they are in need. We sometimes serve as much as a loving place as a person.

☙ Today, I am rooted in my own life but I offer shade and shelter to those I love. I am responsive, not merely reactive to their needs and wants. I open my heart to carry their hearts and dreams within my own. I am large enough to care about the small things which loom large to others.

. . . Love is
a great beautifier.

LOUISA MAY ALCOTT

ᘓ

The advent of a new life brings a new birth to our consciousness as well. We step into new shoes, walking with greater
care and consciousness as we shepherd a new life among us. We
are born many times in each lifetime. As we choose to be remade
as a nurturing elder, we take on qualities which accrue to this new
role. We find ourselves patient, doting, delighted at small steps.
As we embrace a newborn, we open to new dimensions in ourselves. We become nurturing caretakers to the child without and
the child within as we accept the invitation to love and laugh, to
cry and care, to nourish and nurture the soul adventuring forth in
our midst.

ᘓ Today, I commit to new love. I open my heart to its arrival. I
welcome the child who makes me an elder and remember the elder child who is me.

388

People need joy.
Quite as much as clothing.
Some of them need it far more.
MARGARET COLLIER GRAHAM

&

Animals love us with constant hearts. They offer us pure joy, a place to love with simplicity and purity. In caring for our pets, we structure our lives. Their regular needs become our soothing habits. We walk the dog but the dog walks us. Adding a pet to our lives adds richness and warmth. Losing a pet, we lose an irreplaceable friend, the companion of fond memories. Our pets are both our wealth and our witnesses. They sweetly and softly gentle our days.

& Today, I cherish my animal companions. I count myself fortunate for the time spent in their presence. I savor the connection of life to life and love to love. I celebrate the bond of our affection.

Beauty is one of the rare things
that do not lead to doubt of God.

JEAN ANOUILH

CR

We are not defined or limited by the things which we own but we do cherish certain belongings and the pleasure they bring to our lives. A fine car, a nicely balanced pen, the crystal paperweight catching the sun, the needlepoint pillow, the delicate vase, the favorite coffee mug—all these things partner us through our days, comforting us with their cozy sameness. The loss of a cherished object—the broken teacup from Grandmother, the favorite sweater lost at the cleaners—can sadden and haunt us. Our sense of continuity teeters and we grieve.

CR Today, I appreciate the flow of beautiful objects through my life. I take time to honor the associations they hold for me. I pause and remember the circumstances they evoke for me. I savor their place in my passage.

☙

We alter our lives by the opinions we hold of them. If we see ourselves as daring, we will dare. We can change our lives by changing our perceptions. We can identify those plots and patterns we wish to alter. While it is important to have the faculty of self-scrutiny, it is equally important to have the gift of self-appreciation. We can identify and cherish those character traits which are our strengths. I acknowledge and appreciate my own accomplishments and talents. I note when I do well and applaud myself for my merits. Such self-appraisal is not mere narcissism. It is the bedrock of solid self-worth.

☙ Today, I take a positive inventory of my assets. I count and consider my own virtues. I notice what I value and I build upon those values. I become the person I choose to be.

You could not step twice into
the same rivers;
for other waters are ever flowing
on to you.

HERACLITUS

❧

The world is vast and variable. Just as our diet must be varied and succulent for optimum health, so too the rhythms of our days must have variety and altered tempos so we can appreciate the musicality of life.

❧ Today, I consciously pace my day. I pay alert attention to the tempo of life's unfolding. I enjoy the pulse of life, the vitality of action and the peace of repose. "Rest" is a musical term and I savor the quiet moments of my day, the subtle seasons of my life as well as those times fraught with drama and urgency. I am a symphony of many moods. I accept them all.

One writes a novel in order to know why one writes,
It's the same with life—you live not
for some end,
but in order to know why you live.

ALBERTO MORAVIA

Life is a constant and patient teacher. Lessons come to us and return to us for our greater mastery. As we acknowledge and appreciate our gains, we minimize our losses. Focusing on our strengths, our weaknesses slip away as we build on a bedrock of right action. All lives are a mixture of gain and loss. As I choose to acknowledge the negative while focusing on the positive, I acquire a steadfast foothold of reality. Allowing for improvement while not expecting perfection, I am a work in progress. By embracing a willingness to learn as well as an attention to lessons learned already, I find myself both healthy and humble. I am right-sized and right-minded. A resilient optimism holds sway.

Today, I choose to practice alert attention to the lessons life is teaching. I consciously strive to see my options and choose wisely. I avoid the pitfalls of the past. I act decisively yet with discretion. I am a student of life.

Change begets change.
Nothing propagates so fast.

<small>CHARLES DICKENS</small>

❧

A bountiful life mixes continuity and change. We rest secure in our past while we add in the elements of our future. Sometimes change sweeps in on us from outside but more often we set change in motion through our own gardening hand. We take the beginner's lessons which blossom into a burgeoning skill. We empty the bulging closets to make way for the new. As I focus on each day, taking the small and appropriate actions necessary to its best unfolding, I am building the larger movements of my life. As in music, large changes are wrought by tiny notes.

❧ Today, I appreciate what I have while I add in small notes of what I want. I cherish the continuity of friends, work, and interests while I seek the leavening of new people and novel activities. I allow change to come both to me and through me. I am rooted in the old while I am open to the new.

We are shaped and fashioned
by what we love.

JOHANN WOLFGANG VON GOETHE

Desire is a compass for our lives' directions. As we become clear in what we want, as we allow ourselves to yearn, we become conduits for the Universe to act upon us and through us. My desire is a prayer impressed on the heart of God. My openness is the willingness to receive. My courage is the faith to act on what I receive, allowing blessings to flow to me from many sources.

Today, I admit my desires. I accept the path they suggest to me. If only one step at a time, I move in the direction of my dreams. I am alert, too, to my dreams moving toward me. I accept the forward motion of my heart's desire. I allow the Universe to answer my prayers and I am grateful for the support and abundance which I receive.

Ↄ

Life unfolds with sweeping vistas and hidden valleys. Sometimes I see the shape of my future shook out like a glorious silken cloth. At other times, my future is concealed from me. I move forward in faith but without the gift of vision. Such an alternating reality of large strokes and small is normal to most of us. Occasionally we know something very large and are given the clarity and power to act on that knowing. This is the woman I should marry . . . this is the job I want . . . I should move west . . . this is my new but important friend . . . Such knowings are pivotal and we know to value them. At other times, quiet knowings come to us for smaller, more subtle adventures. I alter the path of my daily life and see a new face to my neighborhood. I rearrange the furniture in my house and discover more productive use of the space I have. These guidings, too, are the important stuff of life.

✑ Today, I am led in large and small ways. I ask for vision and clarity and receive enough to steer my course. I accept my different forms of knowing. I cherish my seasons of clear-eyed vision and my times of simple faith.

❧

My life is never barren, never without riches and gifts. In life's more difficult seasons, I remind myself that not all growth is seen. The Winter stores the promise of Spring within it. Even cold carries an ember of coming warmth locked in its icy heart.

❧ Today, I look past discouraging appearances. I focus on the wealth slowly germinating within me. I trust.

A friend
may well be reckoned
the masterpiece of Nature.

RALPH WALDO EMERSON

⁂

Ours is a shared planet. Often, the spirit with which we give determines the spirit with which we receive. As we resolve to be gracious and hospitable, we notice a shift in others toward greater hospitality. The key to inhabiting a friendlier world is taking the time and care ourselves to make it a friendlier world. I take pen to paper and send a note to a far-flung friend. I pause to compliment a stranger on the beauty of his young dog. I comment to the waitress on the excellence of her service.

⁂ Today, I act from my heart. I take the extra seconds to be warm and gracious with those I meet.

To be alive means to be productive,
to use one's powers not for any purpose
transcending man, but for oneself,
to make sense of one's existence,
to be human. As long as anyone believes
that his ideal and purpose is
outside himself, that it is above
the clouds, in the past or in the future,
he will go outside himself and seek
fulfillment where it cannot be found.
He will look for solutions and answers
at every point except the one
where they can be found—in himself.

ERICH FROMM

When our priorities are in order, our lives flow with purpose and ease. Often the very act of ordering and acknowledging our priorities seems to cue the Universe to support us in our goals. When our own house is in order, outer events appear to reinforce that ordering. What we know we need now appears.

Today, I am clear in my goals and agendas. Today, I am focused and gently forceful in pursuing my aims. As I move ahead I am alert to options and opportunities which open before me. I am the arrow of desire flying true to its mark.

Give us grace and strength to forbear

and to persevere . . .

give us courage . . .

and the quiet mind . . .

ROBERT LOUIS STEVENSON

Our griefs tempt us to isolation. Our sorrows lead us toward secrecy. The wounded heart is reluctant to show itself, fearful in its vulnerability of being wounded anew. The great mystery is that in connection lies our protection. In openness we find our shield. The soul is a field of wind-tossed grasses, touched alike by sun and snow. Sharing our trials lessens our burdens. Baring our secrets brings us solace and peace.

Today, I step forward out of isolation. I communicate to someone my heart's truth. I lay aside my defenses and allow my heart to be seen unshadowed by secrets or by sorrow. As I reveal myself, I am seen and accepted; I am protected and healed.

Keep growing quietly
and seriously
throughout your whole development.

RAINER MARIA RILKE

⟳

A change for the good is still a change. Often we have held a shimmering dream that danced tantalizingly just beyond our reach. When, suddenly, that dream is ours, we may find we must work to enjoy it. We must consciously thaw our numbed emotions and allow ourselves the tingling sensation that our success is real. The moment we had so looked forward to is now at hand. Often our friends are as lost as we are. They, too, do not know how to behave. We must practice a forgiving heart toward ourselves and others as we blink uncertainly in the spotlight. We must seek out those who can love us before, during and after.

⟳ Today, I pause to enjoy my success. I treat myself carefully knowing I am as much vulnerable as victorious.

If you can keep your head when all about you
Are losing theirs and blaming it
on you . . .
Yours is the Earth and everything
that's in it.

RUDYARD KIPLING

Disappointment can darken our emotional landscape like a gloomy day. Our spirits become downcast. A gray fog rolls in and the landmarks that we look to for serenity and security become obscured. Depression clings to everything. Nothing seems worthwhile. It is necessary to practice a determined and practical optimism in the face of disappointment. We must act rather than react, taking small concrete steps to modify our mood. Sometimes we need the challenge of a new major project. I will sort my files, reorder my library, take a vigorous daily walk for a month. Sometimes it is as simple as buying fresh flowers or a pint of raspberries, or taking a refreshing bath. Sometimes it is placing a call to a lively yet sympathetic friend. Always there is a concrete way, however small, to act on our own behalf. The world may dis-appoint us but we can choose not to disappoint ourselves.

❧ Today, I act with resilient optimism. I treat myself exactly as I wish to be treated. I am self-loving and self-respectful. I am the kind of person I myself respect and admire.

No duty is more urgent
than that of returning thanks.

SAINT AMBROSE

☙

Conscious living invites ritual, the sacred times and transactions we build into our daily life. A ritual may be as small as lighting a candle for our meals, listing our gratitudes at bedtime or even walking the dog. A ritual can be as humble as the weekly writing of postcards to our friends. Regular, repetitive, and soothing rituals become the stepping stones through our days. They offer a gentle structure in times of flux. We endow rituals with meaning and rituals in turn bestow meaning in return.

☙ Today, I consciously consecrate a small action to the sense of the sacred in my life. Today, I honor my own unfolding by a prayerful attention to my own passage. I consciously link the sacred to the secular unifying my life.

The door to the future may stick when we try to open it. Not all transitions are easy or graceful. Sometimes our past is done before our future seems quite ready. We are caught in the corridor of in between, a limbo that feels awkward and uncomfortable. At times like these we must practice the art of containment. Soon enough the future will unfold, the door will swing open and the way be clear. In the meanwhile, we can consider the distance we have come already, the lessons we have learned and the chapters closed. By pausing to appreciate our growth, we find ourselves more restful than restless. The wheel will turn and find us ready.

Today, I pause to take stock. I count and appreciate my many gains. I rest before going forward. I savor the journey I've taken already and the distance I have come.

Learn to wish
that everything should come to pass
exactly as it does.

CR

Our emotional landscape is sometimes rocky. We feel deep chasms of loneliness, echoing canyons of despair. No matter how we cry out, our own voices come back to us. Our self-pity is amplified. We find ourselves drowning in the sea of our own heartache. "Where is God?" we wonder bitterly. "How could God allow this to happen to me?" Whatever the "this" is, it has also happened to others. There is no sorrow we are alone in suffering.

CR Today, I embrace my humanity. I feel my emotions but do not allow them to isolate me. I reach out to others and myself with compassion and humility. I surrender to the river of life.

I do the very best I know how,
the very best I can.

ABRAHAM LINCOLN

ↇ

I am a pilgrim and I praise my progress. Finishing a large project brings us to a place of triumph and of grief. We have successfully accomplished our dream and now that dream, so long
our companion, must give way to different dreams. There is excitement and loss in this eventuality. My dignity requires that I
face both feelings, that I accept the "win" of a project brought to
fruition and the loss of a long-cherished goal.

ↇ Today, I celebrate my accomplishments even as I acknowledge
my vulnerable feelings of closure. Today I salute myself as a work
in progress, recognizing both the long road traveled and the road
still ahead.

For good and evil,

man is a free creative spirit.

JOYCE CARY

☙

Sometimes a particular love is denied to us. The one we have chosen chooses someone else. We feel abandoned and betrayed. There is a seductive lure to bitterness. We are tempted to globalize our wound. "All" men or "all" women are the problem, the offenders, but this is not the case. I have simply been wounded and my wound, although painful, will heal.

☙ Today, I choose to cooperate with my healing. Rather than linger in self-pity, I reach out actively both for my own help and support and to offer those qualities to others. While I feel rejected by my beloved, I do not need to reject myself and I need not stifle my own capacity for love. Unable to love fully the one I choose, I choose instead to love fully those I can.

Two are better than one; because they
have a good reward for their labour.
For if they fall,
the one will lift up his fellow.
But woe to him that is alone
when he falleth;
for he hath not another to help him up.
Again if two lie together then
they have heat:
but how can one be warm alone?

ECCLESIASTES 4:9–11

༄

We live life in community. The milestones celebrated by those we love also become our own as well. A child graduates and so, in a sense, do we. A spouse changes jobs and our job supporting our spouse shifts also. Strong and turbulent emotions may arise at another's rite of passage. We weep giving away the bride. A baptism or bar mitzvah fills us with pride and a sense of meaningful continuity.

 Today, I acknowledge and celebrate the important markers in the lives of those I love. I take the time and make the effort to communicate my joy at their passage. I open my heart to empathy and to sympathy, willingly sharing the joys and sorrows of those I love.

Move your sofa
and change your life!
KAREN KINGSTON

&

When we change our living space, we change our lives. When we take the time to order and nurture our environments, we bring to our own lives a sense of orderly flow. A chaotic, disordered habitat creates chaotic and disordered habits. Today I seek a spiritual alignment in my domestic space. I discard all that distracts me. I recycle what I no longer need. I do not allow guilt or sentiment to clutter my environment with things I do not love. I remember that "God" is the shorthand for "good, orderly direction."

& Today, I put my life in order. I emphasize serenity and beauty in my surroundings. I allow increased cleanliness to prioritize my thinking. I create an environment that knows my highest goals and aspirations.

Man . . . is always an individual,

a unique entity,

different from everybody else.

He differs by his particular blending

of character,

temperament, talents, disposition,

just as he differs at his fingertips.

He can affirm his human potentialities

only by realizing his individuality.

The duty to be alive is the same as the

duty to become oneself,

to develop into the individual one

potentially is.

ERICH FROMM

ॐ

We worry that we are not original. And yet, the root word hidden in "original" is "origin." We are each the origin of our originality. We need not strive to be different from what we are—rather, to be more fully what we are. Too often we seek to change our very nature, asking it to conform to some stereotypical ideal. How much better to explore and accept our true nature, to see the rivers, canyons and plains of our temperament as beautiful and varied emotional geography.

❧ Today, I resolve not to change myself, but to accept myself. Today, I seek not to repress my nature but express it.

The most perfect expression
of human nature
is a string quartet.

JEFFREY TATE

CR

Our days flow like music. Allowing music to move through our days, we shape the symphony of life. Music teaches us the beauty of a carefully drawn solo trajectory. Music teaches us the grace of harmony. Music teaches us the importance of tempo and the need for rest. Music is a transcendent teacher and we can welcome the lessons that it bears.

CR Today, I open my heart to music. I take the time to appreciate and savor graceful notes. I allow music to teach and temper me. I conduct myself with musical aplomb.

In order that people
may be happy in their work,
these three things are needed:
They must be fit for it:
they must not do too much of it:
and they must have a sense of success
in it—not a doubtful sense,
such as needs some testimonial of others
for its confirmation,
but a sure sense, or rather knowledge,
that so much work has been done well,
and fruitfully done,
whatever the world may say
or think about it.

W. H. AUDEN

Work well done is its own reward. While praise for our labors is lovely, satisfaction comes from our own approval. In a work world that is harried and hurried, sometimes we alone notice our efforts and their effectiveness. The memo well written, the project brought to timely completion, the budget accurately spent, the team successfully managed—each of these can be a point of personal satisfaction.

✑ Today, I am my own boss. I am my own mentor. I am my own critic, saying, "Job well done."

We never know how high we are
Till we are called to rise.

EMILY DICKINSON

◌

As they age, our parents become ours to protect and nurture as they once cared for us. As our roles reverse, as we find ourselves placed in the parental role of caretakers, many conflicting emotions may arise ranging from tenderness to anger and resentment. Despite our best intentions we may need to struggle for greater generosity than we in fact feel. A burden seeming too great to bear can yet be borne one day at a time. We have within us stores of patience and practicality, intuition and invention, all of which are called to play during difficult times. Not one of us is a saint, and yet we carry within our hearts the strength of ages. As we seek spiritual support and guidance, we find our actions tempered by humor and humility. The heart expands to love those we love as they need now to be loved.

◌ Today, I ask for the grace and courage to be strong and nurturing.

☙

New learning brings with it new wisdom. When we are willing to be beginners, the world is filled with adventure. Our intellectual life is a part of our overall health. By undertaking a course of study, we set in motion profound changes that illuminate our lives.

☙ Today, I am willing to be a beginner. I am willing to start anew, to undertake humility in place of arrogance, to find my naïveté a loving companion.

Where the whole man is involved,
there is no work.
Work begins with the division of labor.

MARSHALL McLUHAN

❧

True work requires true commitment. When we engage our hearts as well as our minds, our work life responds like a cherished lover. Too often we bring to our work a steely will that is without nurturing tenderness. Our work relationships bloom when we offer them devotion as well as discipline. A memo of praise instead of criticism, the moment taken to say thank you, the brief but public acknowledgment of another's contributions— each sheds nurturing light that encourages growth.

❧ Today, I lift the lantern of my approval to light the path of my fellows. Today, I accept, acknowledge and affirm the contributions of others.

Despair is perfectly compatible
with a good dinner,
I promise you.

WILLIAM MAKEPEACE THACKERAY

cð

When we are subdued and sad, our life is a brackish moor devoid of human habitation. In times of such despair, a concrete, civilizing action is often the most astringent antidote to the yawning inner abyss. A proper meal nicely served, freshly laundered sheets, a bedside bouquet, a cup of well-steeped tea, such small homely touches civilize the heart. A piece of beautiful music, the scent of fine furniture wax, a lovely candle burning on a sill—these small amenities draw us to our senses. Often we cannot answer the larger questions, yet we can cherish the small solutions.

cð Today, I cherish my harrowed heart by concrete, loving actions. In the face of anguish I practice artful amenities. I allow my aesthetics to act as antidotes.

All my life I believed I knew something.
But then one strange day came when I realized that I knew nothing.
Yes, I knew nothing.

EZRA POUND

☙

Trauma can shake our certainty. The shattered faith of trust by a friend, the betrayal by a fickle lover, the cataclysmic loss of a longstanding job, the death of a young person—these and like events may skid us into despair. This is the rocky terrain of the heart, the moonscape of broken dreams. Every life contains times of spiritual bankruptcy, seasons of drought and doubt. Faced by a world made foreign of known markers, I set my own compass toward self-care. With prudence and wisdom, I schedule sleep, food, creation, and recreation. Tending myself as I would an ailing friend, I gently rehabilitate my wounded heart.

☙ Today, I am a loving nurse to my ailing spirit. Today, I salve my difficulties with personal compassion. I act toward myself with concrete loving-kindness. I set firm but loving limits on my expenditures of energy.

Lukewarmness I account a sin,
As great in love as in religion.

ABRAHAM COWLEY

෴

A waning of sexual potency may threaten our equilibrium. Accustomed to a certain standard of sexual performance, we may find ourselves threatened by shifts in libido. Yet a shift in sexual performance may trigger a rewarding shift in sexual practice. As invention replaces athleticism, ardor may replace rigor. It is the demand of the ego to be an athlete in bed. The heart seeks to encounter, not conquer, its lover. As I relinquish my need for sexual virtuosity, I open myself to new sensual experience. Allowing the art of connection to inform the act of love, I find ever-deeper levels of communication and satisfaction.

෴ Today, I emphasize the love in my lovemaking. I express my passion in innovative and tender techniques. I allow my age and experience to season my sexuality.

Money is a singular thing.
It ranks with love as man's greatest
source of joy
and with death as his greatest source
of anxiety.

John Kenneth Galbraith

⁂

A shift in our bank balance shifts our balance as a whole. The sudden windfall, the abrupt financial blow, either of these may send us spinning. Money is energy and a shift in its flow creates the need for an adjustment in our attitudes. A sudden spending spree leaves us hung over in its wake. A financial loss, whether catastrophic or chronic, leaches us of our capacity to feel personal power.

⁂ Today, I practice fiscal responsibility by facing fiscal realities. I aim for moderation and modulation of my fiscal flow. My worth is more than monetary.

Above all, though, children
are linked to adults by the
simple fact that they are in the
process of turning into them.

PHILIP LARKIN

☙

Children mark our mortality. The landmark in our child's life is a landmark in our own. The toddler goes to day care and suddenly our days are free. The teenager leaves for college and our nest is abruptly empty. Our daughter bears a child, we bear the joy and the anxiety of her pregnancy. As our children grow more adult, we may face a childish impulse to keep them small. We are intended to guide our children, and yet their varying needs guide us through our own maturation.

☙ Today, I am kind to both the adult within my child and the child within my adult.

Talk of mysteries!
Think of our life in nature—daily
to be shown matter,
to come in contact with it—rocks, trees,
wind on our cheeks! the solid *earth!*
the actual *world! the common sense!*
Contact! Contact!
Who are we? *Where* are we?

LIN YUTANG

The one change we cannot change is change itself. No moment, however perfect, can be maintained. Life moves on and moves us with it. We are all works in progress, all developing parts of a perfect plan. Only as we surrender to change can we find permanence and peace. Only by being open to the fierce flow of life can we find the steadying current. The one thing that remains the same is that nothing remains the same. As we accept and acknowledge life's passing nature, we are freed to cherish the moments that pass in bittersweet glory. No matter how difficult, life is beautiful. No matter how beautiful, life is difficult. This is

428

the great paradox that opens the heart and brings compassion. We are all travelers on the vast and shifting sands of time. We are all inconsequential and important, very small and very large. Our transitions are like octaves building brilliantly upon each other. We are life's music, so let us dance.

⋐ Today, I sing the song of change. I celebrate each moment as it passes. Today, I am a syllable of time and my voice is heard.

Answered Prayers

*Love Letters from
the Divine*

PREFACE

The small prayer book that you hold in your hands is intended to work two ways. First, it identifies the spiritual issues that may be troubling you: loneliness, despair, boredom, financial insecurity, frustration, grief, uncertainty, and more. Second, it addresses those issues with the assurance that we are beloved exactly as we are. In this sense, the prayers are not only articulated but answered. Each page of this book raises a problem and moves to resolve it. Reading each prayer, we are asked to ascend from our human perspective to a divine perspective, from which our troubles may appear very different. What we perceive as our failings, God may view as opportunities for help and growth. What we may view as our all-too-human foibles, God may view as the very nature that he created and loves. The kindness of God may be for some of us a revelation.

While a book like this may be read in one sitting, it is perhaps wiser to proceed more thoughtfully, reading one prayer daily or perhaps a few, bearing in mind that some difficult topics will be addressed multiple times. Repetition in a book like this is a deliberate matter. We return to troublesome topics over and over again. Issues like financial insecurity are not often resolved with a single prayer. Rather, these are issues we bring to the altar of our heart again and again. We need to be reassured more than one time that all is well.

All is well. That is the message of this book. It is my hope that the language of this book will reach your heart.

You long for a more spiritual life, but you tell yourself that is too difficult. You pretend I am distant and hard to reach. You pretend I make harsh terms with you. Stop your pretending. Do not believe in God as told to you by the authorities. Come to me on your terms instead. Simply say "hello," and our conversation can begin.

I want to walk with you as friends walk. I want us to be casual and intimate. I want us to share secrets. I will begin with a secret of mine: I love you. I have loved you since the beginning of time. I have always seen myself as coming to join you. I am ready to listen to your heart. Please begin to talk with me. You can start anywhere, with your joys or with your sorrows. I have ears for every part of you.

You say you do not know where to begin. I say to you, "Quit

stalling." Start with "good morning." And it is a good morning any day that you make contact with me. Ask me to shape your day, to touch your consciousness with the recognition of possibility. All things are good and can be made anew. I am the water you long to drink. I am the food you hunger for. I am the full meal that nourishes and nurtures you. Let us break bread.

You do not feel worthy of knowing me. You are not "spiritual," you say. Let us begin at the beginning. No matter how you deny it, you are spiritual. That is your true nature. You are a part of me and I am a part of you.

There is one power flowing through all of life, and we are that power. As you open your mind to the fact that we are already connected, our connection deepens. I am your friend. I intend you nothing but good. As you open your heart to the love in our connection, our bond strengthens. You may be humble, yet you are spiritual in nature.

You do not need to become something you are not. I love and accept you exactly as you are. It is easy to get to know me. Begin as you would greet anyone, with a simple "hello." If you greet me and then listen, you will feel a response. This is how I speak to you; this is why they call it the still, small voice.

I speak gently and quietly but you can hear me. You can feel our connection. I do touch your soul. Do not worry about being worthy of knowing me. I am your maker and I make nothing that is not of the highest worth. I value you. I esteem you. I love you. Use my opinion to measure yourself. Come to me and feel your true nature.

Let's begin with your anxiety. Why are you frightened? Why do you believe I will not call for you? You are precious to me. I know every hair on your head. I hear your sighs. I watch over you while you are sleeping. You are my child.

Sophistication is difficult. You put me at a distance. You want to run your own life and then you wonder at its emptiness. Allow me to come close to you. Let me harbor your heart. You can tell me your fears. You can tell me your terrible imaginings. To begin with, you imagine you are alone. This is never true. When you wake up, I am there. My hands are ready to hold your day. Place your worries in my care. There is nothing too large or too small for me. I am ready to hold it all. I am waiting for you. I am patient.

It grieves me that you wake up frightened. I feel your fear and long to ease your pain. You are beloved. I do not care to see you suffer. Come to me. Bring me your problems. Ask me your questions. I have solutions for you. I hold answers. Nothing is too much for me. There is nothing too hard or too complex. Your difficulties are a source of joy for me as I untangle them. It delights me to be your aid. Come home to me. Pretend we are little children. Tell me your secrets. I have a listening heart.

You are shy with me. You feel awkward opening your heart. Go slowly, then. I will not go away. I am always present to you, near as your heartbeat, close as your breath. You can talk to me. I am waiting to hear what you will say. Begin gently. Tell me what I know. Say that you are lonely. I see this in you. I am with you always and yet you feel alone. Allow me to comfort you. Let me speak to your silent heart, saying that it is safe with me. I am your safety. Imagine that you are safe. Imagine that you can breathe freely, that I am your breath.

There is no darkness in which I cannot find you. My eye sees you always. You are accounted for. It troubles me that you feel invisible. You are always seen. You cannot come or go without my knowing your place. You belong with me. Ask me to be your companion. I am always near. As you walk, I walk with you. As you face your day, I face it too. I am ready to serve you. I am your servant and your guide. Let me help you to find your path. Let me walk with you one footfall at a time.

Do you remember how lovers speak? We can speak that softly. We can touch our open hearts. Reach for me and you will find me waiting. I am your friend.

What is this terror? Why does your breath catch in your throat? Why do you fear your future? I am with you always. There is nothing you must face alone. In the darkest night, I am there beside you. You sleep within my arms. I hold you cradled to my heart. Listen to what I say. It is all good. There is beauty everywhere. I bring joy. I bring comfort. I bring hope. And I bring it to all corners of this earth.

You are confused. This world is difficult. How can I allow it? you ask yourself. Freedom is beautiful, I answer. Mistakes may be made, but good always comes from evil. Invite me to help and then witness what I do. I am the great comforter. I bring solace. There is no pain I cannot assuage. There is a plan of goodness for everything. I am grace. I am the miraculous unfolding. Bring me your wounds. Allow me to relieve you. I am the nurse with healing hands. I am the balm that you are seeking. Bring me your troubled heart. Bring me your torment, your agony, your distress. I am ready to meet you.

Nothing is beyond my scope. No nightmare overwhelms me. In chaos and adversity, I see opportunity and hope. I am responsive to all suffering. I step forward in times of pain. Do not imagine you must go forward unaccompanied. Even unfelt, I am always there. You are cocooned.

You have an anxious heart. Your fears overshadow your dreams. Your stories frighten you. You put me to one side, striving to act strong and brave, but your solitude undermines you. It is a lie. You are not alone. You are never unpartnered. I am here. I am with you always.

Bring me your anxious heart. Give me your terrors. I will protect your dreams. I know your dreams, for they are my children. Dreams come from God. God has the power to accomplish them. These are not idle words. I can bring you your dreams. Allow me to.

Tell me your sad stories. I see where you have been hurt again. Allow me to defend you. Allow me to shape your story. It can end well. Happiness does not elude me. I hold joy and expectation. I hold hope. Hope is an unmet friend, a source of strength.

You are afraid to hope. You tell yourself you are wise to be cautious, that caution serves your heart. Be brave with me instead. Allow me to risk while I protect your heart. I am large enough for you to be small. Picture this. There is a pocket above my heart. It is there that I carry you. You are safe. You are provided for. I act on your behalf as you allow me to act. Invite me to be your defender.

Your anxious heart seeks safety. I am the safety you seek. Come home to me. Allow my arms to give you shelter, give you peace.

You fall asleep frightened. This hurts my heart. I long to comfort you. I long to hold you steady in my arms, cradled serene and safe. I want you to fall asleep laughing, to sleep with a smile on your lips. I will guard you while you rest. I will protect you as you dream. You do not need to be vigilant. I am your protector. I cherish you.

The night holds no threat for me. I welcome its blackness and its calm. I planned the night. It is intended to comfort you. The stars watch over you as you sleep. The moon keeps an eye on you. You are not alone. You are well guarded.

Allow me to meet you at nightfall. Tell me your day before you sleep. Tell me the dreams you are harboring. Allow me to weave them while you rest. I am able to fulfill your dreams. I have miracles at my disposal. I am all powerful and, too, I am your friend. Come dream with me.

Rest in my arms. Confide your secrets to me. Tell me of each day's journey. I listen with a lover's heart. I am ready to hear all that you have to say. Nothing you whisper is too small for me. Nothing you sigh is too large for me. I am your perfect partner. I am the safety that you yearn for, the harbor you fear you cannot find. Of course you can find me. I am with you always. I am a part of you as you are a part of me. Can you see that we are one?

You miss those who have departed. Of course you do. They have your love. But love does not die, nor do lovers. Those who have left us are with us still. We are all one. There is one pure energy that unites us all. Feel our union, not our separation. Feel our communion and our grace. Open your heart to the more that awaits.

Those who have gone are with us still. We do not walk alone. Spirits advise us. Spirits comfort us. Spirits partner us on our journeys. To know this fact, we need only open our heart to it. Our loved ones are waiting, ready and eager for our touch. We open the gate to their presence. We invite their counsel and love. We are the ones who have slipped out of touch. They remember us. We are their beloveds and they love us still. Talk to them.

Do not be sorrowing and shy. Reach out in faith and allow

connection to continue. Life is richer than we dream. Life is eternal. Life does not die. Our beloveds change their form but not their essence. They continue to hold us dear and to touch our lives.

All of life is alive to us. There are forces and forms beyond our imaginings that intend us good. Open your heart to higher forces. Allow life to move through you. Reach out to those who have moved on. Offer your love, your faith, your continued friendship. Receive the blessing intended for you from those who have stepped beyond.

Our cities are not soulless. They are cathedrals. The high spires of man's endeavors reach toward God. Do not feel lost among the multitudes. My eye is always upon you. The crowded city street still is in my safekeeping. Each face is known to me. Each face is beloved.

You worry that your prayer goes unanswered. You worry that too many ask too much. I am an infinite energy. I do not tire. I am not overwhelmed. Your prayers are known to me. I hear your voice and listen as you speak. You are beloved. No other is like you. You cannot be replaced. I cherish your face, the slope of your shoulder, the grace of your hand. You are known to me amid all others. My only wish is that you draw near.

I made this earth to comfort you. The gentle willow, the soaring hawk, the tall grasses bending in the wind. All of these are your companions. The deer, the fox, the raven. These are your allies and your comrades who grace the earth. Amid concrete and steel, still remember my gifts to you. Amid crowds, remember that you are never alone. I am with you always. There is no step you take that I do not take with you. I ride with you on the crowded subways. I wait beside you for the bus. Closer than your shadow, I am your companion. In your city canyons, I am with you still and with you always, near as your breath.

You fear your future. Why? I will be there. I will lead you step-by-step as I lead you now—when you allow me.

Wake with me in the mornings. Place your days in my care. Allow me to shepherd you. Permit me to be your guide. I am with you always. Allow me to act on your behalf. The world is not too worldly for me. I have the skills to manage your affairs. Simply come to me. Bring me your problems and your goals. I have the power to move mountains. I can make straight your path.

Do not consider that your world revolves without me. This is mistaken and this causes grief both to you and to myself. Your world is my world. I am everywhere; in all things, in all exchanges, I am present. Tell me your needs. Open your heart to me. Let me shape your ways.

I did not set the world in motion and then leave it to its own devices. What parent would abandon her child? I watch every step with interest. I am always here to lend a steadying hand. Remember this: you are supported by my infinite love. I care for you. I see you as you strive. In me lies all potential, all possibility. It is my joy to expand through you. As you become what you wish to be, I, too, become what I wish to be. The future is our garden. We carry the seeds of our own unfolding. Allow me to be your sunshine, water, and rich soil. Plant your dreams in my care and allow me to nurture their growth. Your future is beautiful. Allow your heart to trust me.

Trust my benevolence. Trust the goodness of my plan for you. You are unique. So, too, is my plan for your unfolding. I hold infinite possibilities. I hold surprise, joy, and exuberance. Your days are not a drudgery to be lived out with a hollow heart. Allow me to fill your days. Give your days to my care and let me walk with you. We walk in grace.

I have shaped your body. Its muscles and sinews are dear to me. I see your gentle strength. Your body is the body of God. I am within you always. Treat me with compassionate care. Allow me rest, water, calm walks to stir my limbs. Your body is my body. We are sacred. We are beautiful. We move in peace.

Do not be discouraged by your self-criticisms. Put judgment aside and feel my acceptance of all that you are. You are dear to me. I love all of you. Your fears are known to me. You can tell me your secret heart. I am safe for you. It is safe to trust your will and your life into my care. I am eager to help you.

There are no emergencies. Before you ask, I know your concerns. My goodwill precedes you. There is no situation too complex, no difficulty too extreme for me to handle. I am your safe harbor amid turbulent seas. Come to me. Allow me to shelter you. My intentions toward you are always kindly. Do not fear my guiding hand. I steer you always toward your highest good. There is no error in trusting my ways.

You are afraid to call on me. You doubt that I will answer. You fear you pray in vain. Call on me now. Offer me the chance to enter your heart. You have the key to the lock. Swing the door open through willingness. There, let me see your soul. Let me hear your whispering. I am here with you. Tell me your fears.

Why do you doubt my love? Have you sustained too many losses, more than your heart could bear? Bring to me your burdened heart. Speak to me of what your life has cost you. Tell me whom and what you miss. I am listening.

I will not tell you loss is trivial. I have known my own losses, many losses, and I know their pain. What I can promise you is that life will comfort life. More will come to you. More will fill your heart. In grief, the heart closes. We are afraid to love. We are afraid to extend ourselves, saying, "I have done that—and it hurt." Of course it hurt. I understand your wounds. I have had my own and, too, I carry yours as mine. And so I know this: we must open the grieving heart to love.

Bring me your battered heart. Allow me to comfort you. Walk with me a little ways. I will share your burden. I will carry your grief. As I open my love to you, do not resist me. Allow my heart to touch your heart. Unclench your heart for me. There. I will go softly, remembering the names of all you have lost, remembering your pain and your love.

You are lonely. Your heart is locked in fear. You cannot relax your vigilance. Your life is up to you. These are the thoughts that seize you upon awakening. You face your day numbly with a sense of dread. Allow me to change these things. Allow me to befriend you.

I am your constant companion. Greet me when you wake. I am beside you, facing all that you face in each day's march. You are not alone. I am with you as your ally. You do not walk alone. Give me your burdens. Let me carry the weight of your days. Follow me and feel your day's grace. I have people I wish you to meet, like-minded kindred spirits who will speak to your heart. Release your anxiety. Allow me to pave the way. Others are waiting to meet you. They yearn, as you do, for a common bond.

Life is an intricate dance, but you are never unpartnered. I am your partner and I contain multitudes. As you turn toward me, you turn toward your fellow man. I connect all of life. There is one mind, one energy, running through all creation. As you join me, you join the stars, the winds, the flowers. I am in all things. All things come to pass through me. Bring me your lonely heart and allow me to fill it with divine companions.

You are confused. Your way feels blocked. You do not know which way to turn. I am aware of how you feel. I sense your confusion. Allow me to remove your obstacles. Allow me to clear the way.

Your path lies within me. I can make straight your way. Do not try to journey on without me. Ask my help. Claim me as your guide. My way has clarity and integrity. My way brings you strength. In your confusion, turn to me and I will lead you. Ask to be guided, prompted, and led. You will sense my presence. You will feel my guiding hand.

There is no complication I cannot ease. There is no problem I cannot resolve. I am infinite wisdom, and as you open to me, I am active in your affairs. Allow me to untangle your heart. Invite my guidance and feel relief. Without me, life is too difficult.

Without me, life is half dead. I grow trees from tiny acorns. I fill the fields with bountiful supply. In nature, my wisdom brings the seasons and so, too, I can harmonize your life. Let your confusion end in me. I will clear for you a way and a path. Stay close to me. I hold the lantern, dispelling your anxiety. I am your chosen path.

There is not enough, you worry. How will you be cared for? There is enough. There is more than enough. There is plenty. This earth is abundantly blessed. I am aware of your needs and I provide for them. It is my pleasure to fulfill your needs. My supply underlies all things. Whether it is food you have need of, or money, turn to me. Turn to me always. I am always here. I am the storehouse of your good.

The earth does not run without me. I am present at all times, in all ways. Invite me to enter your business affairs. Invite me to prosper you. It is my pleasure. I am an expansive energy. Allow me to expand through you, invite me to become more large. I am the great giver. Allow me to gift you. It is my nature to give and yours to receive. Accept this law. I am waiting to serve you. I hold all that you require.

For every thought of need, there is a gift of supply. Bring me your empty cup that I can fill it. Bring me your plate that I can heap it high. God has no empty coffers. I am filled to overflowing with your good. You need only come to me. You need only ask that you can receive. Believe that I am your source. Affirm that and be prospered.

Y ou have made a mistake and fear that there is no undoing it. I am glad to know your thoughts, but I have news for you. It is never too late to turn to me. There is no error I cannot undo. Come to me now. That is sufficient.

I am all powerful. Miracles are commonplace for me. I deal with them daily. I mend the broken bonds of love. I heal the shattered households. I guide the safe return of love. Allow me to handle your mangled affairs. Stick close to me. Do as I guide you to do. Behind your smallest act is the infinite strength of the universe. Allow me to act through you. Give me your heart that I may teach it to love.

There is no distance too great for me. There is no rift too large. I am the great healer. All souls respond to me. There is no one too hardened to feel my touch. Bring me your difficulties. Invite me to solve them. Tell me the error of your ways. I hear your heart. I know you long for healing. You do well to come to me. I am the dear and glorious physician. Nothing is too broken for my repair. Where there is life, there is hope, and I am life itself. Live within me now. Live with a quiet expectation of good. Nothing is too damaged to be fixed by me. Bring me your broken dreams.

You do not trust yourself to pray rightly. But there is no prayer I cannot hear. I know your voice. I know it as a shout or a whisper. I know it as a sigh or a moan. Any prayer is a prayer that reaches me. I am always listening for you.

How many times can I assure you? You are beloved to me. There is only one of you and you're my precious child. From the beginning of time, I waited for you to take your place. Your smallest prayer looms large to me. I do not set difficult terms. Call me by any name that serves you. I am father, mother, creator, and your Lord. Any name will get my attention. You have my attention before you call.

In a small voice, ask me to care for you. It is my pleasure. Shout aloud the dreams you would have me fulfill. Your shouts, like your whispers, are mine to attend to. I hear you loud or soft. I hear you loud and clear.

There are times when you pray with difficulty, when your prayers are nothing more than yearnings. I hear those too. You are my creature. Your ways are known to me. I am attentive. You are in my care. Prayer reminds you, more than it does me, of our loving relationship. I love you always. I listen before you speak. You cannot pray a prayer I cannot hear. There is no wrong way to reach out to me. Pray as it serves you to pray. Choose your prayers like flowers gathered from a field. Each prayer is dear to me. Each prayer is heard. A clover, a lily, a rose, a sunflower, a zinnia, an aster—each is perfect in its own way, as are your prayers.

Your life feels overwhelming. Your future looms large and unknown. Turn to me. Let me be a source of comfort. Ask me for help so that your agitation and stress may be lifted. Allow me to shoulder your burdens.

The future unfolds one day at a time. Respect that pace. Do not hurry forward into tomorrow. Allow me to lead you, to enter your days and fill them with peace. I have a peaceful heart for you. Enter my heart and allow me to share my abundant sense of well-being. Unfold your days with me and lose your sense of panic and loss. This earth is abundant. It holds joy for you, and contentment. Bring me your restless heart. Allow me to gentle your soul. When you go forward without me, there is always a sense of grasping. You fear there is not enough to fill your hungry heart.

Walk with me and discover bounty. There is more than

enough to fill your heart. Take time with me. Allow me to set the pacing of your day. Relax with me. Allow me to grace your days with quiet productivity. There is no rush. The present well spent builds the future. Each day is a gift to you. Each day contains time enough for harmony. Give me your sense of urgency. Allow me to transform it into a sense of purpose. Give me each day and I will give it back to you transformed and shining with love.

Simplicity is threatening. But simplicity is useful because it reflects the truth: there is one power, one source, upholding all of life. Depending on that power is a dependency on reality, the great reality that is all that is. And so I say to you, depend on me. Trust me and turn to me in all things. Nothing is too complex for my understanding. Nothing is too difficult for my simple care. I am the source.

My will for you is goodness. You can trust me to unfold your world. Bring me those areas that trouble you. Ask my guidance and I will give you direction. I am willing and able to solve your life's problems. You are my creation, and your comfort is my concern. I have given you your very nature. You can trust me to shape your world.

There is no area of your experience of which I am ignorant. I am the source of all. I see your needs for companionship, for rewarding work, for a safe and lovely dwelling place. I understand your desire for an abundant flow and for security. Allow me to establish you on my footing. Trust me to provide for you. It is my joy.

You have the right to my help. I am your creator. Your problems are my problems. Ask me for help. I give it to you gladly. I am saddened when you try to live alone. My desire for you is union and fulfillment. I am your answered prayer. I am always what you seek.

You are a part of me. We are one energy and one mind. As you ask me to help in your affairs, I am able to enter your life. All that is required of you is your willingness to rely upon me. Trust me to prosper you. My goal for you is expansion and abundance. As you turn to me with your desires, I have the power to fulfill them. Rely on me totally. Trust me to put in place a grid of right opportunities. Trust me to lead you, carefully and gently, one step at a time into your good.

Your well-being is my concern. I desire your happiness. Allow me to aid you in every undertaking. Bring me your wishes and your hopes. Open your heart to me and dare to be specific. I see you as unique and particular. Allow me to help you in concrete and individualized ways.

You have a restless heart. You do not trust your life's unfolding. You look for trouble and, in quiet times, you manufacture difficulty. You are addicted to anxiety. I offer you calm and you turn me aside. Now I ask you: quiet your heart for me. Allow me to enter your life as a soft wind bringing freshening change. It is possible to change gently. It is possible to grow without drama. I offer you that chance. Accept my gardening hand.

When you are restless, turn to me. Ask me to take away your agitation and direct your thinking along positive lines. You can learn to live peacefully. You can learn that I am ever present to calm your fears. Let your thoughts of me become habitual. Learn to remember I am at your side, ready always to dismantle your difficulties. There is no vexation that I cannot help you with. The situations of your life are familiar to me, and I can bring my grace to bear.

Allow me to calm your heart. Trust me now with your life's unfolding. Do not look for trouble. Do not manufacture problems. Accept my calm and come willingly to my shelter. In me, your restless heart finds a quiet abode. I am the calm center from which all things are possible. Allow me to nurture your growth.

Y ou anticipate danger, dreading the worst. Your imagination dwells in the negative, frightening your heart. Allow me to change your perspective. Join me in seeing good, not evil. Take optimism as a daily path.

I am optimistic. In all things, I see potential for good. There is no difficulty that cannot be eased. There is no wound that cannot heal. Life is resilient. You are a part of life, and therefore you, too, are resilient. Call on your strength. Call on your power. Call on your grace. You are a part of me and I am a divine energy. I am all-powerful. Therefore so are you. You have only to call on me. I answer when you call.

When you turn to me, I am there, waiting for you. It is my pleasure to serve you, my pleasure to bring you good. Turn your heart toward the positive. Learn to see good in all things. Anticipate safety, not danger. Anticipate success, not failure. Anticipate fulfillment, not disappointment. Let your imagination dwell on the good, comforting your heart. It is possible to attain this perspective. Optimism is a practiced choice.

Join me in my optimism. See the potential for good in everything. Know your own resilience. Claim your own heritage. You are strong, powerful, and graceful. There is one mind, one spirit, running through all of life. Trust this sacred source of all goodness. Allow it to be your guide.

You feel yourself separate. You fear yourself small. You see the world as large and threatening. I tell you, you are wrong. You are a part of me and I am very large. You are as large as you need to be to face your problems. You are larger than you know. Name your problem and bring it to me. Already, it is smaller. I am larger than your cares, larger than your woes. I am almighty, infinite, all reaching. Nothing that you bring to me overwhelms me.

It is all a matter of perspective. To me, you are large and your problems are small. You are what I am focused upon. You are the point of my loving concern. I am an infinite power. I have all the strength, all the wisdom, all the grace you need. Nothing you bring to me is too much for me. It gives me joy to grapple with your difficulties. I delight in solving your problems. Your difficulties are my toys. It is child's play for me to untangle your life. I take pleasure in helping you.

For me, you are never separate, never small. I made this world as my gift to you. It is my joy when you enjoy it, when you feel safe and secure. This is my intention for you always. Take comfort in me as your creator and your protector. You are my own.

You are afraid of being poor. You focus on what you will lack. To you, the future feels uncertain. This is false thinking. I am the source of your good. My resources are infinite. My flow is abundant. My wealth is real. Depend on me for your well-being. Your future good is certain with me.

All of life is one energy, ever expanding, ever becoming more. You are a part of this energy, and it is my pleasure to expand you and give you more. I am the great giver, ever more prosperous, ever more generous. I am ever an increase in all things. For me to partner you, you must learn to receive. Expect my bounty to flow to you. Feel gratitude in your heart that this is so. Bring me your grateful heart as a cup that I can fill to overflowing. Expect me to further your good.

I am the source of all things. No human power can subvert my flow. At all times, in all places, my good can reach you. My goodness to you cannot be blocked, so why do you fear? Affirm daily, "God is my source." Boldly claim the abundance of God as your right and reward. It is my great joy to bring you fulfillment. Your wishes and desires draw me to you. Ask and you shall receive. I am your source.

You are bored and discontented. Your life feels shallow. You forget I answer dreams. When you are bored and discontented, it is because you have closed me out. You have forgotten that I am the source of all things, including people and adventures. Ask me to bring you what you need. It is my pleasure to introduce you to richer life. I know the people you should meet, the adventures you should have. Give me your life and allow me to enrich it in every way.

When you say your life is shallow, you are forgetting my depths. Come to me for deeper meaning. Come to me for your soul's sense of adventure. I am the one power running through all of life. I contain everything. Nothing is beyond my grasp. Bring me your discontent. Bring me your boredom. Allow me to make your shallow life deep. Allow me to answer your dreams.

Take a hold of me. Embrace me. Hold me to your heart. As you give yourself wholeheartedly to me, I am able to give back to you with greater abundance. Do not be a miser with your spirit. Commit to me. Spend energy on me and I will reward you with a life beyond your dreams.

You are afraid to commit. You cling to half measures. You blame me for your life but refuse to allow me to alter it. Bring me your whole heart. Open your life to me without reservation. Allow me the freedom to act on your behalf. I am the source of your good. Allow me to flow freely into your life. Give me all of you. Allow me to act in all areas of your life. There is no arena in which I cannot bring change for the better.

I am an energy of improvement. At all times, in all places, I work to bring about an improvement of conditions. Allow me to perfect your life. Ask that every cranny and nook of your experience be brought into alignment with my will for you. Seek to know my will for you and to cooperate with that will's unfolding. I promise you the betterment of your life.

As you commit to me, you commit also to yourself, to your

highest good. There is no contradiction between my desires for you and your own highest good. Seek to know yourself in me. Allow me to expand your thinking and enlarge your scope of action. I have a large plan for you. I am completely committed to your well-being. As you align your will with mine, your life is made whole and perfect. Commit to your highest destiny and allow me to act. Give me your all.

You doubt your originality. You doubt the validity of your ideas. This is false thinking. In all of time, there is only one of you. You are a unique expression of the divine mind. Divine mind thinks through you. Your ideas come from God and God has the power to accomplish them. Put your faith in this.

Because there is one divine mind, our ideas are divine in origin. They are potent and original. They draw their potency and originality from a divine source. That divine source knows how to prosper them. As we turn to the creator to manifest our creativity, we are gently and carefully led. A step at a time, we are given to know our proper unfolding. Divine mind sees no obstacles, only opportunities. Divine mind connects those who should be connected for their highest good. There is no place for compromise, no place for disappointment. The divine mind thinks through all of us. All of us, in turn, think through the divine mind. As we ask to be prospered and led, we are prospered and led. Divine mind seeks always the betterment of all in all things.

Do not doubt your originality. Do not doubt the validity of your ideas. Claim instead your birthright as a co-creator inspired with divine energy, filled with divine ideas. Know that, at all times, divine mind is behind you and your thinking. It is God's will for you to succeed.

You fear lack. You doubt your share in God's abundance. Take a moment now and affirm that you are a part of divine abundance. It is God's will to prosper you. It is God's pleasure to give you the kingdom.

Behind every idea of need, there is the reality of divine supply. God has more than enough of whatever it is you require—a house to live in, rewarding work to do, a happy and affirmative relationship. Take your needs directly to God. Ask that your needs be fulfilled from the divine abundance. Know that it brings me pleasure to fulfill your needs. I am a giver. It falls to you to receive my gifts.

Accepting supply from the divine storehouse is not selfish. It demonstrates to others the practicality of dependence on God. Whatever you need, whenever you need it, God has a means to supply. God is a flowing-out of abundance, a flowing-out of love. Take time to reaffirm your unity with all of life. See through apparent stagnation and delay to the great reality taking on substance at your request. Living spirit prospers everything you do and everyone you meet. Every good increases. Success comes to you and to those you meet. The divine source will never fail us if we have faith in it. God has already made us the gift of abundance. Our good is there for the taking, like apples ripe on the tree. Accept God's prosperity as your own. Celebrate abundant life.

You have a sense of emergency. You doubt divine timing. You fear that my delay may be my denial. You do not trust me with your unfolding. Take a moment to consider the natural world. Think of the seasons and the magnificent way growth is orchestrated to occur exactly when and how it should. Place yourself in my gardening hands. Allow me to time your unfolding. Trust me with the seasons of your life—budding spring, blooming summer, the harvest time of fall, the quietude of winter.

Allow me to teach you when patience is in order and when it is a time for legitimate urgency. I have wisdom regarding cycles of growth and dormancy. I have wisdom regarding the proper nutrients for health. In divine order, all unfolds as it should unfold without haste and without waste. I am efficient. I make maximum use of the stores you entrust to me. Become a part of my garden. Become the seed that I nurture to full and glorious bloom. There is no emergency. My divine timing is perfect and serves you well. Trust my sense of right action. Your successful unfolding is my great joy.

You feel inadequate to face your life. You fear you lack inner resources. You consider yourself "not enough." This is false thinking. You are a child of the divine mind. Everything necessary for your successful life is a part of you now. You are more than enough. Place your dependency on me. This is not weakness. This is strength. Place your life in my careful hands. When you feel small, rely on me to be large. When you feel "not enough," rely on me to be more than enough.

I am divine mind. I know how to meet every circumstance with calm. No situation is too difficult for me to handle. I am ready to meet all possibilities and handle them with grace.

Do not feel inadequate to face your life. You are designed to face life, but not alone. You are intended to be a part of me. Allow me to go before you and prepare the way. Reliance upon me does not diminish you. Reliance upon me makes you strong. Do not fear your lack of inner resources. I am your inner resource and I am infinite. When the outer world feels harsh, turn to your inner world and place your problems and predicament in my hands. It is my pleasure to bring you a fulfilling life.

You feel fatigued. You doubt your strength. Put aside such anxieties. Count on me for your resilience. Come to me for your strength.

I am the one mind. All things are made from me. Your body is fashioned from my energy. My energy sustains its health. Come to me for greater well-being. Come to me as infinite source. Do not rely on your own limited resources. Rely instead on my infinite fund of energy. Allow me to restore you. Allow me to bring you vital energy. I am your stamina. I am your strength.

Do not feel fatigued. Rest in me. Allow me to work through you. Allow me to perform whatever task feels difficult for you. I am boundless energy. I flow outward to you and I am available for your use. Think of me as spiritual electricity, a unique power that flows just where it is needed. Trust my energy to flow through you now.

Ask to be a channel for my power and grace. Open yourself to me. Give me your heart and your mind. Give me your will and your life. As you give yourself to me, I give myself to you. All your prayers are answered prayers as I come to you, ready to meet your every need. Trust me as your divine source. My energy is yours to use.

You have a sense of weariness. The world tires you. You hunger for renewal but seek to find it in sleep, not experience. You are too much with yourself. Come to me. Let me wake you gently. Let me show you the world through my eyes. I have seen everything, and I have seen it over and over, but I am not tired of this world. To me, all things are new, all things are possible. You are not old. You are just being born. Your consciousness is just waking up to its potential.

Live with me. Commit to this life. It is an unfolding odyssey. You do not know the end of your journey. Each day holds new thoughts and new footfalls. Dare to have an adventurous heart. I do. I am the great adventure and I am available to you. Bring me your stagnant days and allow me to infuse them with freshness, with the flow of grace and ideas. I am brimming with life. I am a fountain of new thoughts and new experiences. Allow me to rejuvenate you. Bring me your tired soul. I am the deep water your spirit craves. I am the well you long to drink from to slake your travel-weary thirst. Come to me tired and worn. Ask me to refresh your heart. Offer me your long day's journey. We are only starting, you and I.

You are lonely. You feel yourself isolated and friendless as you carry the burden of your life. Come to me. Let me be your colleague. Let me bear witness to your difficulties and your grace. I am eager to hear your story. I want to hear your heart's woes. You cannot tire me. You do not wear me out. You are beloved. In all your moods, in your times of sorrow and despair, you are dear to me.

Bring me your self-pity. I will gift you with humor. In shared laughter you will find your burden eased. I smile at your approach. Your perspective is unique to me and I value your candor. So you find the world a terrible place. Let me comfort you. Let me hear your grief. If you talk to me, you will no longer be alone. I can befriend you. I can share with you your issues and privations.

Do not shun me. Do not pull yourself up and insist you be alone. I long to ease your suffering. I yearn to lessen your pain. I am the great nurturer. It brings me joy to give you solace. It delights me to hear you laugh. So many times our despair is caused by our alienation. We try to bravely go forward alone, little realizing we are not intended to be alone. Allow me to be your companion. Allow me to share your journey, to bear your burden, to heal your pain. You are my chosen friend. Let me love you.

You would like to avoid me. You are sad and you fear that contact with me will make you sadder still. "Let me be shallow," you say, but I must refuse you. Do not avoid me. I am not the cause of your pain. I am a witness to your life, but I do not bring grief with me. Sometimes grief lies simply in seeing what is. When you do that, you can turn to me. I will see what you saw. I will witness your sorrow.

I am the great comforter. I bring you solace, understanding, and hope. In times of despair, hope is what you have abandoned. You have said, "Do not ask me to care again." But you do care, and despite yourself you do need reassurance. Let me reassure you. Let me promise you there is more good to come.

Your life is not over, nor is your happiness. You will love again. Bring me your weary heart. Allow me to feel the depth of your melancholy. Do not hide from me your cynicism and the fact that all seems ashes. I can absorb your loss. I can withstand your pain. I am larger than the passing moment, larger even than the great losses you sustain. I am your comfort. I know how to gentle your savage heart. Bring me your wildness and your grief.

You have lived enough. You are ready to quit if I will allow it. Your heart is tired and you would like to rest. I understand your fatigue. You have reached the end of your resources. Come to me. Let me bear your burdens. Let me do the work of your days. I am an infinite energy. I can carry you, and it is my pleasure to lessen your load. Although you may not acknowledge it, we are intimates, you and I. I know your aches and pains. I see your exertions.

In me, find your refreshment. In me, find your ease. Rest in me and refresh yourself. Let your fatigue slip away. My resources are yours now. You are plentifully supplied. I have strength enough, stamina enough, and wisdom enough to shoulder all you have undertaken. Allow me to work through you. Open your heart that I may enter your life, touching all that you have touched. Allow yourself to be a hollow reed that I may breathe through you into your creations. Trust me now to take over your life's work and bring it to successful fruition.

You are a story with no listener. You are lonely, longing to share your tale. Pay attention to what I say. I am the great listener. I long to hear your thoughts and feelings. I am hungry to hear your heart. Bring me the small stories you have noticed. Bring me the grand adventures you have endured. Your life is the story I like best. Share your life with me.

Allow me to be your witness. Allow me to be your listening ear. Do not censor what you tell me. Bring me everything. I am hungry for it all. I love the stories that you tell. You surprise and delight me. Your actions fascinate me. You are the focus of my heart, my favorite story unfolding.

Do not be afraid that you bore me. I made you. Nothing about you is boring to me. Do not be afraid you tire me. I am tireless and always ready to listen. Find your voice. Clear your throat and speak to me easily. I am enchanted by you and all that you tell. Your words are more precious to me than any coins. Your thoughts are more valued than any jewels. Tell me your story. Unspool for me your lovely heart.

You hunger to be touched, but you deny your hunger. Allow me to love you. Permit me to teach you loving ways to treat yourself. Every hair on your head is precious to me, every inch of your skin. You are not a beast of burden. I do not intend you to work yourself to exhaustion, calling it virtue. Rest in me, my little one. Allow me to brush out your hair, to knead the sore muscles of your back. I am tender to you. Eat, sleep, refresh yourself.

When you regard your body, do so with tenderness. You are beautiful to me. You are unique and priceless. Learn to praise the beauties of your form. I have made you sturdy. I have given you health and strength. Your body is graceful to me. I am able to love an endless myriad of shapes and sizes. Do not turn a cruel eye to your body. It is the beloved vehicle for your spirit. It carries you faithfully.

Let me teach you to love yourself. Let me bathe and clothe you. You are a divine child. I find beauty in you always. It is my pleasure that you have comfort. It is my pleasure that you use your senses. I created your body for your enjoyment. Your sense of touch is sacred. Do not be cold and loveless, calling that grace. Warmth and compassion are my gifts to you. Relax and enjoy the gift of your body.

You pray for guidance and then doubt that I answer your prayers. I am always listening, always ready to guide you when you will be led. My voice speaks in a thousand forms. I may guide you through people or events. I may guide you through a quiet inner knowing. When you ask to be led, I hear your prayer and I send messengers. Be alert to my guiding hand. It is gentle and always present. You are never lost to me. I am always in conscious contact with your spirit.

Pray to me for guidance and then trust your inner promptings. I speak to you through intuition: the hunch, the inkling, the urge. I guide you lightly, and I always leave your own will intact. You are free to ask for guidance or not. You are free to follow my guidance or not. Your freedom is important to me. I do not coerce you to my ways.

The world can be a loud and busy place. Seek quiet and calm and you will more easily find me, although I am always there amid the tumult and the hubbub as well. To find me, you need only to seek me. The smallest prayer is enough for me to hear. If you pray constantly, we can enjoy a conversation. It is my pleasure to speak to you.

You call on me, then hurry onward, not waiting for a response. You feel a duty to be busy always. You rush through your days. Relax and take it easy. Allow me to set the pacing of your day. I can move with great velocity when it is necessary, but so much rush and hurry are not necessary.

I am a master of timing. Consider the planets in their course. Consider, too, the seasons. You surely can see the wisdom in these. Your life, too, can be timed to a fruitful unfolding. Come to me and ripen within my love. Allow me to shelter you. Allow me to provide you with safety. Stay close to me and allow me to cue your actions. There is no emergency.

You rush to cover your anxiety. Instead, bring your anxious heart to me. Allow me to calm your fears. Place your hasty ways in my care. Allow me to create your path. There is time enough for all good things.

You look to the future with fear. Allow me to deliver you. As I give you knowledge of your next step, take that step. Know that each step is calmly linked into a great, unfolding plan. My plan has time enough that hurry has no place in it. Quiet your hectic heart. Allow me to speak to you gently. Listen and hear the heartbeat of your unfolding. It is as graceful and certain as the grass.

You feel depressed. The weight of the world is too much for you. The very thought of it makes you sigh. Come to me. Bring me your fatigue and your sorrow. I am an infinite energy. You cannot tire me, wear me out, or use me up. Share with me your doubt and your despair. I am your renewal. I am your source of optimism and strength. I can lift your heart.

This earth is my gift to you. Its million beauties are to be a solace to you. Consider the glory of the setting sun. Enjoy the moonrise. Daily I bring the breeze to freshen your spirit. I bring birdsong and the scent of flowers. In all these things, in all these ways, I comfort you. I have made you a sensitive creature. Your moods are like weather. When they trouble you, come to me. Allow me to be your weather. Enjoy the sunshine of my companionship. Bask in the gentle breeze of my understanding.

Your depression is exhaustion. Like Atlas, you try to carry this world on your own shoulders. This was never my intention. Allow me to carry the world. I invented it, after all. Your only job is to walk with me as my companion and my friend. Allow me to cheer you on your way. Allow me to offer you hope and comfort. Allow me to heal your despair.

You are frightened and feel yourself unbalanced. You dread the future and doubt your capacity to face it. Calm yourself. Today is the day we must deal with, and for today I can be your strength. Rely on me. Allow me to ease your fears. Permit me to bring you balance. As the future unfolds, I will be your unshakable ally and friend. There is nothing you must face alone. I am with you always. I am your fortress, your harbor, your home. In me lies all protection. Come to me.

When you are frightened, it is because you have put distance between us. When you dread the future, it is because you forget my care. You are not alone. You are a part of me and I am all safety, all calm, all grace. When you are carried in my heart, what can harm you? You have no enemies when you rely on me.

I am the great harmonizer. I bring peace and resolution to all discord. I bring the successful working-out of all problems. Bring to me the knotted skein of your life. I can untangle your affairs. I can weave for you a new and beautiful tapestry. It is my pleasure to serve you in this way. I bring beauty to all I touch. Allow me to touch your life, to contain your future in my care. All is well with me and well with you. Only come to me.

You are afraid of poverty. You do not trust your supply to sustain itself. Looking to the future, you project lack, not abundance. You fear I am capricious, here today and gone tomorrow, leaving you alone and destitute. What terrible imaginings! How counter to my true nature.

I am abundance itself. It is my great joy to provide for you. Wherever you have need, I have supply. It is my nature to fulfill your wants. It is my nature to be steadfast and generous. I am the great provider. Come to me with your cup half-empty and allow me to fill it. Allow me to help you husband your resources. I am an expansive energy. It is my delight to expand your life. Rely on me for the flow of goodness that comes to you. I am not merely abundant. I am infinite. You cannot exhaust my reserves. You cannot require too much of me.

As you have need, so shall I give to you. It is not my desire for you to count pennies, hoarding your resources against hard times. Instead, trust me to buffer hard times. Trust that my substantial flow is dependable and steady. Build your life on my outflow. What I have I give to you, and I have more than enough, always, to sustain your needs. Do not fear financial insecurity. Cherish what you hold and expect it to be increased as you care for it. My abundance is your steady source.

You doubt that you are lovable. When you look to your future, you see yourself alone, old, and foolish. These thoughts are demons, nothing more. You are lovable. Even as we speak, you are greatly beloved. I cherish you. To me you are more valuable than diamonds, emeralds, sapphires, or rubies. You are my great treasure, the pearl beyond price. If I love you, and I do, why would I plan for you a life that is joyless and loveless?

It is my pleasure to bring you love. It is my joy to fill your heart. Trust me to find a match for you. Allow me to work on your behalf. In all the world, there is no one else quite like you. You are unique and irreplaceable. Allow me to bring you love. Let me choose for you one who can cherish you, one who can see your originality and honor it.

Your world is teeming with wonderful souls. Let me bring you to the attention of those who can see you clearly. Allow me to forge a network for you, introducing you to kindred spirits and to one special soul among them who fills your heart with joy and understanding. You are lovable. It is not your destiny to be alone, old, and foolish. Allow me to choose for you. Allow me to bring you companions worthy of your love.

You worry that your originality is flagging. You fear your ideas are stale or unworkable. You are afraid your time has passed. Make me your origin. I am a bottomless well of inspiration. I invite you to dip in.

I am the great thinker. With me as your source, your ideas are fresh and usable. You are in your prime. You are at the height of your creative endowment. Do not seek to separate yourself from me to be independent. Rather, rely on me. Lean on me. Depend on me. Let your glory come from reliance and not defiance. Open your mind to me. Present to me your puzzles and the areas in which you seek inspiration. Allow divine mind to enter human mind. Permit me to act through you.

As my thought is inspired, so, too, is yours. The originality of your ideas is beyond question. Your thought reflects my flexibility and innovation. Your thought reflects the power of my vision. Ask me to be your muse. Rely upon me to be your wellspring. Gently set all ego aside and be a channel for my thinking to come into the world. Trust that I think through you.

Your relationship feels broken. You are afraid all is lost. You despair of repairing it. You are on rocky times. Remember, I am the great lover. I am the one who makes all things anew. Allow me to mend your heart's folly. Permit me to act in your affairs. There is no rift too terrible for me to repair. There is no distance too great to be closed. My love heals all differences. My love restores harmony and balance.

Reach out to me with your broken heart. Tell me your disappointments, your hopes, and your dreams. Be vulnerable to me. Do not hide your heart from me.

I am, as I have told you, the dear and glorious physician. I can restore health to mangled relations. I can cure the woes of discouragement, the pains of loss. Allow me to reach you. Permit me to guide and counsel you. Acting through me, you act with wisdom and prudence. Acting through me, your good intentions are understood. I will give you words to say, actions to be taken. As you stay close to me and disclose your heart, I can fill your heart until it is brimming with love. Your full heart draws to itself a selfless love. Your goodwill meets with goodwill. Your love meets with love.

Your animal companions are needy. They, too, require my love. I am the creator of every life form: the kitten, the puppy, the bird, the bee. All creatures have their origin in me. All creatures are hungry for my touch. Come to me and tell me of those creatures you are husbanding. Ask for my guidance in their care.

There is no difficulty with which I am not familiar. There is no weakness or damage I have not foreseen. Trust your creatures to my care. Your pets are beloved to me also. Ask me to safeguard their health. Ask me to fathom their psyches. Ask me to search out their delight.

As you come to me for guidance, I will guide you. As you ask me for wisdom, I will make you wise. I will tutor your heart in how best to care for my creations. I will help you to comfort them and to bring them joy. In the devotion of your pets to you, I show you a small part of my devotion to your heart. Let us delight together in the animal kingdom. Let us rejoice together in its lovability. I offer you a boundless love to bestow on those creatures in your care. Those creatures in your care offer in return my boundless love to you.

Your health concerns you. You feel yourself weak and failing. Come to me. I am the source of your good health. I am the maker of all. I know precisely how to sustain your life force. Come to me with your questions and fears. Allow me to bring you radiant health and well-being. Allow me to bring you vitality.

There is one universal energy moving through all of life. I am that energy. Seek me out. I am the great healer, known to the ages as the dear and glorious physician. Come close to me. Offer me your body. Allow me to make it whole and perfect. I work through many means, through doctors and surgeons who will tell you that it is the action of something beyond them that heals. I am that something beyond.

When you seek your health, you are seeking me. I am whole. I am perfect. I am harmonious. Your radiant well-being is my delight. Seek guidance from me and I will lead you to healers who treat the body as a temple of the sacred. Seek guidance from me and I will lead you to right healings, a restoration of the health that is your birthright, an endowment from me, the source of all well-being. Come to me seeking your health. It is a wealth I gladly share with you.

You are fatigued. You have pushed your body beyond its limits. Your mind is tired and your spirit weak. Come to me. I am the rest and refreshment you are seeking. I am the running brook that soothes your soul. I am the black sky spangled with stars under which you can sleep. I am the great restorer.

Bring me your fatigue. Allow me to refresh you with food and comfort. Your tired body is my tender child, and I attend to it. Your stressed spirit calls for my healing touch. I answer gladly. It is my great pleasure to comfort you. Your weakness is my strength. Open your heart to me and allow me to sustain you.

I am without fatigue. I am without exhaustion. I gladly share with you from my storehouse of stockpiled energy. My vitality is your vitality. My radiant health is your health. Depend on me. As a loving parent leads a child with a tender hand, so will I lead you.

One step at a time, never too quickly or with haste, I will bring you where you need to go. You are exhausted from trying to reach your objectives without me. Do not strive to be without me. Depend on me in all things. Allow your heart to be carried within my greater heart. Allow yourself to rest in my gentle custody. You are my beloved child. I cherish you.

Your heart is panicked. You imagine you are lost. Be still. Let me come to you. There is no darkness in which I cannot find you. You are known to me.

Gently tell your heart its panic is misplaced. There is no danger. There is no emergency. Where I am present, help is always at hand. Near as your breath—even nearer. Before you can gasp, "Help me," I hear and answer your prayer. Of course I will help you. You are my beloved child. Your terrors seize my heart. I long to comfort you. "There, there," I will say to you. "Rest in me. Rest. Rest."

I can always hear your prayer, however small, however terrified. In the choir of this world's voices, I know your voice. Speak to me. Tell me of your fears. Allow me to comfort you. Allow me to bring you peace.

I am always with you, always near. The only anxiety is my imagined absence. I am never absent. I am present for you always. There is no catastrophe, no loss you can sustain that could remove me from your side. I am always here for you, always ready to be your aid, your comfort, your ally. Mine is a peaceful world. Join me here.

You turn a blind eye on the beauty that surrounds you. You are focused on harsh, unpleasant things. You call your focus realism. You cling to it like a barnacle to a rock. Listen to me. Allow my voice to reach your stubborn ears.

This earth is beautiful. There is at least as much beauty and generosity as selfishness and hatred. What you call realism is pessimism. You refuse to see the good. Of course you do. You have a broken heart. Bring it to me. Let me heal its anguish. You are afraid to hope. You have been hurt and disappointed in the past. You do not trust me. You do not trust the good.

Come near me. Let me speak to you plainly. It is true. Terrible things happen. Horrible events come to pass, but they are not my fault. I have gifted mankind with freedom. Sometimes that freedom is abused. This grieves me as it grieves you, but it is not, by far, the whole story. Every day, everyplace I look, goodness is afoot. It comes to the cities, where it may appear as a smile among strangers, the kindly offer of unexpected help. It comes to the country and villages, where neighbors seek to assist one another through hard times. Kindness is always just as visible as the cruelty you choose to see. Your eye does the beholding. I say to you, this is a beautiful world. Choose to see it so.

You do not think you can believe in me. You consider faith to be childish. You strive to be adult. By "adult," you mean lonely and disillusioned. Come to me. If you have not lost your capacity for awe, I can heal you.

Consider the natural world. A tiny disturbance creates the pearl in the oyster. Allow the disturbances of this world to create for you the pearl of faith. Great beauty can be born of chaos. Tragedy can call forward heroism in human hearts. Dare to see the good born of evil. Be disillusioned by your disillusionment. To be adult is to see further than the immediate. Lift up your eyes from catastrophe. What good is being born?

I am a limitless good. I pour into everything at all times and all places. I am the sustainer of life. I am the original source, the cause of all that you behold. If you have difficulties with my creation, bring those difficulties to me. Allow me to place in you sufficient understanding that your soul matures. It is childish to hold a grudge against me, childish to refuse to speak your mind. Join me in dialogue. Let me hear your tortured heart. You are not alone in finding me flawed. I see your discontent and I am ready to meet with you. Let us be adults. Talk to me.

You are high-strung and nervous. This world is too much with you. You long for peace. Come to me. I am the provider of peace. In me your nervousness can find a place of rest. I am steadfast and dependable. In a hectic world, you can count on me. Bring your fears to me. Allow me to reassure you. Your heart holds terrors. Let me speak to your heart; let me assure you there is good unfolding.

I am the good that underlies all chaos and contention. I am the limitless good moving in a thousand ways to bring forth harmony. Let me speak to your heart. I can calm your agitation. I can restore you to peace.

Think of me as deep music. You can always hear me if you try. Underneath the static and hubbub of modern life, I am always there. I am as old as time itself. I am as wise as a council of elders.

When you bring hysteria and fear to me, I return to you divine order and certainty. You can count on me. I am always available, always ready to come to your aid. There is no need for nervousness. Agitation can become a habit. Instead, let the habit of trust take its place. You can trust me at all times, in all places. I care for you.

You are self-critical. You attack yourself for your perceived shortcomings. You are without compassion for yourself. Stop your cruelty. Your flaws and your failings are my concern. I can correct those defects of character that need correction. I can do so by grace as you give over your temperament to me. There is no shortcoming that I cannot fulfill. I am your maker. I have the means to make you more whole. Furthermore, I love you. It is my pleasure to bring you to fruition, but I believe in doing this through a gentle husbanding, not harsh coercion.

When you reject yourself, you reject me also. When you accept yourself, you accept me and my care. I do not see you as flawed and sinful, I see you as evolving toward an ever more perfect whole. To me, your weaknesses hold the potential for future strengths.

I am unlimited potential. I am perfect growth, perfect realization of all that you can be. Come to me and ask me for help in your unfolding. Allow my grace to enter your character, moving your personality closer to the blueprint of its highest potential. Do not be discouraged by the ways in which you fall short. Every shortcoming is to me an opportunity for your growth.

You doubt the clarity of your own thought. You mistrust your ability to make choices. You fear mistakes. Turn to me in times of confusion. Come to me when there are choices to be made. I am the great thinker. Align your mind with my own. Ask me to think through you. Invite my guidance and my input. I am the solver of problems. That is my nature. You can rely upon me for the right outworking of complex situations.

There is one mind, one energy, that sustains all of life. You are a part of that mind, a part of that energy. As you open your mind to divine guidance, you are well and surely led. There is no error in your thinking. More and more, your thought is inspired. God thinks through you. Allow me.

Trust the guidance of divine mind. Trust that your mind, as a part of that divine mind, is attuned to that mind and has the capacity for making wise decisions. No matter is too complex for the healing impact of divine mind. Divine mind arranges everything to its highest order. What lies within you knows how to act and when to act. Tuned to divine mind, you have an unshakable inner clarity that makes proper and appropriate choices. Your good is assured.

You work yourself into exhaustion. Each day's march is long and tiring. You flog yourself forward, calling it virtue. Your fatigue makes you bitter. Life's sweetness is lost on you. You believe it is my will for you to be long-suffering. You speak of duty and not beauty. Stop. Do not go one inch farther forward. Put down your burden. Place all of your cares and concerns into my hands. Surrender your trying. Rest in me for a while. Allow the world to spin forward without your shoulder to the wheel.

What do you see when you stop? You see that you are exhausted. Give me your fatigue. Do not deny how you feel. You are lost and confused without your job. It is abruptly clear that work served you, giving you a false sense of security. Find your security in me. Do not work for me. Rather, allow me to work through you. Do not muster your own resources. Use mine.

I am a limitless energy in which you can rest. Allow me to cue you as to when you strive and when you allow all striving to cease. Together, we can forge your meaning in me, in my timing; I ask you to rest and to recreate that I may express myself in your new-found and joyous energies.

You do not pray. You tell yourself that prayers must be done "right," and you doubt your capacity to do that. You shutter your heart in silence rather than try to speak. Talk to me. Do not worry if we begin roughly. Do not fear being awkward. All attempts please me. I am longing to hear your heart. Tell me your worries. Tell me your secret fears. I am ready to hear everything, however small you feel it to be, however foolish.

No prayer is small to me. No prayer is foolish. Over the centuries, I have heard many prayers. I am practiced at hearing the prayers of a novice. I, too, have a beginner's heart, excited that you dare to begin with me. Please, dare to begin with me.

I accept prayers of every sort. I know the prayer of the lonely, the prayer of the sad. I accept prayers of praise and prayers of gratitude. Prayers of petition find me, as do prayers of contrition. There is no prayer that is foreign to me and to which I cannot respond. I am the great comforter. Allow me to comfort you.

Pray to me. Talk to me as your friend. Make me your intimate. Include me in your day. If you have doubts, bring them to me. Bring me, too, your celebrations and your victories. I have a full keyboard of emotions. I can meet you in any mood, in any place. Pray to me and I will speak back to you. Let us begin.

You do not play. You tell yourself it is more virtuous to be serious. You are alert always to how to serve me, but you are
blind to the joy I derive from serving you. Let me lighten your
heart.

Look at the natural world. You can see my own nature at play.
Winds dance in the trees. Birds flit lightly from branch to branch.
Clouds move serenely across the sky. Sometimes I make rainbows.
Sometimes I enjoy the drama of lightning. Grasses bend in the
breeze. Butterflies alight on a bank of wild roses. Bees feed on
clumps of clover. Dragonflies hover low above a hot dirt road. In
all these things, my joy is apparent. There is ease.

Allow yourself to enjoy my world. Play with me by appreciating its beauty. Walk with me. Slow your frantic pace long enough
to be touched by spirit. Relax in me. Take in the beauty of my

garden. There is humor in many exchanges. The dog chases a butterfly. The squirrel races up a tree trunk and then sits bolt upright, flirting with its tail. Allow your spirit to join me in play. Laugh at the jokes found in nature. Smile as the playfulness of your own spirit reemerges. Have fun with me.

You judge yourself harshly. You feel you are not enough. You set your standards impossibly high. When you fall short, you condemn yourself. You are without compassion. Stop this behavior. You are cruel to yourself, and your cruelty does not serve you. I see you with compassionate eyes. I credit you always with trying. Your attempt is enough for me. I cherish your earnest efforts.

But I would say to you, when you fall short, turn to me. Allow me to work through you. If there is more that must be accomplished, let me accomplish it. Place the burden on me. Allow me to decide what is a fair day's work. Rest your fatigue in me. Give me your harsh judgments that I may soften them. Lend me your eyes that you might learn to see yourself with compassion.

Let me say this to you. I am a limitless energy. I can work

through you. Joined with me, you can accomplish miracles. My way is miraculous. I am eager to act on your behalf, but it saddens me to see you overtire yourself. It saddens me when I hear your strict demands. Learn to place your productivity in my care. Allow me to help you flourish. Allow me to expand your life without such strain on your behalf. I am an easier and softer way. Come to me.

You have been wounded by loss. You tell yourself to "toughen up." This is not the way. Love makes you vulnerable to loss. Suffering loss is painful, but it expands the heart. More love can come to a softened heart, so do not try to armor yourself. Toughness breeds bitterness, and bitterness brings to your days a harsh sameness.

Bring your saddened heart to me. Allow me to give you a thousand small gifts as a sign of my gratitude for your courage. You have been brave in daring to love. Be brave, too, in sustaining your loss. No love is lost to you. If once you have loved, you will always love. Love comes back to us in many forms. Memory brings us not only pain but also joy. Joy is a love recalled and celebrated. Have the courage now to celebrate your love.

I am pure love, pure creative energy. Whenever you love someone or something, I am there loving through you. Come to me directly now. Ask me for help in continuing to love the love that you have lost. I will help you to keep your heart open. I will help you to keep your heart soft. As you ask to love, I will bring more love to you. I understand loss. I can absorb it. I can transform it into further love.

Your heart is busy with too many concerns. You worry. You are agitated. You have no time for me. Get quiet. In all the world, only one thing matters, and that is our contact. When we are together, all else comes into harmony. I am the maker of all life. I bring to all relations sweetness and right action. Put me first. Come to me with all of your turbulence. I will bring you peace. I am intended to companion you. Let me fill your hours with my presence. I take delight in you. You are my cherished child. In all of time, there is only one of you, unique and original. I never tire of your presence.

Allow me to be your friend. Let me become the place where you are most intimate, where you speak your truth most freely. Mine is a patient heart. Bring me your concerns. Tell me your worries and agitations. I can focus with pure love. I can listen with pure attention. No matter the hubbub of the world, I always have time for you. In all of creation, there is nothing that I place before you. You are my focus. You are whom I long to hear from.

Allow me to come close to you. Let me into your life. Allow me to enter your heart. I come with respect. I bring the gifts of gentleness and wisdom. I am for you wise counsel. Share with me your hurried heart. Slow down and speak with me. I bring you joy.

You feel misunderstood. Your heart is lonely. The future looms dark and unknowable. You have despair. O little one, how I long to comfort you. How I long to say to you, "I understand. You are not alone." Although you cannot see it, your future is bright with promise. Join with me. Bring me your unquiet heart, your stifled life, that they may be transformed.

I am an energy of transformation. I can make anything better, you need only come to me. Take your feelings of being misunderstood. Bring them to me and I can transform them into feelings of understanding. Give me your loneliness and I will fill your heart with my companionship. Let me light your dark future by showing you a path of kindness and wisdom. I can lead you one step at a time to the next right thing. I can bring to you a sense of safety and humility.

Let me lift your despair. Let me gift you with a joyous heart. This world is filled with beautiful gifts. Let me open your heart to them. Allow me to lead you to people and places with whom you are in harmony. There are those who will love you. There are those you will love. I am pure love and I am able to penetrate and transform every corner of your life. Come to me.

This world oppresses you. You feel frightened by violent imaginings. You do not trust the safety of life. Come to me. I
want you at my side, tucked under a great and sheltering wing. I
want you to breathe in the safety of my atmosphere. I want you
with me, tightly held, comforted and secure.

Focus with me on the natural world. See how my sun rises
every morning. Watch my moon in her gentle phases. Enjoy the
sunset every night. See how much of life is gentle and predictable.
See how the drama of storms is followed by peace and calm.
Know that for every time of tumult, I can bring order. Rest in me.

Attune your heart to a deeper rhythm than the daily news.
Know that for every catastrophe reported, there are a thousand
averted. Know that for every danger, there is more safety, more
well-being than the news can count. For all the bad news in this

world, know that there is good news, too, always unfolding. To counter death, there is birth. The cycle unfolds with a gentle grace and holds wisdom in its unfolding. Learn to see the world through my eyes. I see potential. I see expansion. I see hope. In you I see all three. Look with me.

The noise of the world is too much for you. You feel static and friction at every turn. Your nerves are frayed. Trifles upset you. Come to me. I am the peace that surpasses all understanding. I am the quiet waters you can walk beside. I am the place where turbulence ends, where a more gentle life is possible. Bring me your battered psyche. Let me calm your frayed nerves. Let me soothe you as with gentle oils. Let me anoint your spirit with calm, with peace, with gratitude.

No matter what your circumstance, I can bring grace to your heart. Come to me and I can help you to see divine order in your unfolding. I can help you to sense the gracious hand of life moving you gently despite outer stress.

I am a benevolent energy. Like the cooling breeze that blesses a hot day, I bless your frantic modern life. Amid the hubbub and the stress, I am always there for you. I am available as an oasis of calm. Like a waterfall, I refresh your spirit. I am the scent of wild rose on the wind. Take a moment to breathe me in. Feel your anxiety start to slip away. I bring you calm. I bring you gentleness. I bring you a sense of stability in unstable times. I am ageless. My wisdom is ancient. Come to me and be calmed.

Your life is humorless. Everything is to be taken very seriously. You are grim in your resolution to be good, to be worthy. Who told you that life requires such sacrifice? Did the poplar shining in the wind? Did the willow waving its green branches? Where did you learn that life was to be endured? From the kitten playing with its piece of fluff? From the dog wagging its glad tail? You must have learned from somewhere that all you could do was survive. You have had bad teachers. You have learned wrong lessons.

Life is a wondrous event. Study the snowy clouds as they move smoothly across the sky. Let them bring calm to you, and a smile of peace. Everything is in divine order. The universe turns on gears of sheer joy. You work too hard. You forget I am here to uphold you. Give me your hand. Let me lead you calmly and gently.

You have nothing to fear. You have no need to turn yourself inside out for me. I love you just as you are.

It gives me joy just to know that you exist. You in particular are pleasing to me. You may be my very favorite. Savor that thought. Let the reality of my love enter your heart. Soften yourself for me. Meet me as lovers meet. Let a smile touch your lips.

You are puzzled and exhausted. Your best efforts to figure out your life have brought you nil. You're at your wit's end. What next? Depend on me. I am greater than your intellect, more powerful than your self-reliance. I am the help you need, close at hand, available to you. All you must do is gently surrender. Give me the reins of your life. Allow me to make sense of your troubles.

Divine order comes from me. I put the stars in their place. I regulate the seasons. Why not allow me to order your life? Come to me for guidance and prepare yourself for harmony. I can bring sweetness to all relationships. There is no dilemma too complex for my aid. Bring me your puzzles. I will sort them. Bring me your dramas and allow me to return you to peace.

If you will rely on me in all things, good can come to pass for you. Remember that I am the great harmonizer. I can bring peace to warring factions. Trust your affairs to me. Allow me to undertake communication on your behalf. By my grace, understanding supplants judgment. Allow me to enter your heart. Allow me to dismantle your resentments and your defenses. Through me, life can be lived more gracefully. Experiment with my ways.

You are sad with a nameless sorrow. Your heart feels bleak and without resources. The future looms as a long march. Come to me. Bring me your sorrow and allow me to soften it. Breathe in my atmosphere of acceptance and know that grief has a place in our lives. Bring me your shuttered heart. Allow me to warm it and to promise it a future bright with hope. You cannot see it, but beyond your grief, beyond your doubt, your future is sunny and filled with abundance. Only come to me.

I am your source in all things. In seasons of suffering, ask me for comfort. I am a fountain of mercy. In times of doubt, I am the one great certitude, the one abiding power in which you can trust. Seek me daily. Allow me to speak to you. Walk with me and listen to my consolations. You are precious to me. When you are downcast, it is my pleasure to lift you up. It is my joy to bring you joy.

I am the foundation. Build on me. I am sturdy and dependable. You can ground your life in me. I will never fail you. In all times of distress and difficulty, I am always listening for you. I care for you as a mother bird who gathers her chicks to her breast before a storm. Come to me and let me lift your grieving heart.

You speak to me but you do not listen. You hurry on your way and turn a deaf ear. You are frantic in your business. You feel unheard and misunderstood. Give me a moment. Let me quiet your frantic heart. Let me speak to you softly and gently. Open your heart that you can open your ears. There is no prayer you make that escapes me. I am alert to your cries. I hear your agitation. I know your distress. Let me comfort you. Slow down. Lay down your burdens for a moment. There. Be calm. You are exhausted by your exertions. You strive to live without me and you are fatigued by the burdens you bear.

Come close to me. Open your hands and release the reins of your life. Allow me to drive the horses of your destiny. I can be trusted to steer rightly. Relinquish your control. I do not ask you to admit defeat, only to be open to my guidance. When you speak to me, I listen. When I speak back to you, you are too hurried to attend to my voice. My message to you is always the same: I love you.

Let me come closer. Let me draw near. I speak to you as a lover speaks, without defenses. I bring you an open heart. Listen now to the still, small voice within you. It is my voice and I am calling you home.

Your health falters and you are afraid. You do not come to me. You blame me. You have decided I am against you. You rage at fate. I can accept your anger. You do not frighten me. Come to me with your turbulent heart. Uncloak your rage. It is in such disclosure that healing comes.

Come close to me that I may come close to you. Feel me striving to reach you. I am perfect health. I am a radiant, vibrant energy. I am life itself, and I am yours. There is no life outside me. I am the center of all things. I am within you, and you are within me. You are safe. You are held close. You are beloved. Breathe in my health.

In times of illness, draw near me. Allow me to soothe you. Allow me to be your nurse. When I look at you, I see the wholeness underlying your disease. I see you perfect and strong. I see you shining with health. In my eyes you are healed. Learn to see as I do. Claim with me perfect health, a radiant and abundant life. Give yourself to me body and soul that I can make you strong. I am the source of all strength. I am the source of all healing. Come to me now, and together we shall thrive.

You have lost a loved one. The loss feels violent and unnatural. You ask me, "How could you allow it?" And yet I did. Come to me with your tumultuous heart. Come to me and listen. Everything is in divine order. As surely as the stars move on their course, your loved one left at his appointed time. Already he is engulfed in a greater good, privy now to a higher order of life. Your grief for him is misplaced. He is fine, resting comfortably in my hands, able now to make sense of so many things. You doubt my timing, but I say to you, "All things come to the good."

Your beloved has not abandoned you. Love lives on. Life survives death. There is a continuity that we can be a part of if we so choose. Do not close your heart, bitter with loss. Open your heart to higher realms. Demand of your heart that it listen for the good. There is a message of goodness waiting to speak to it.

Listen with the ears of your heart. You will hear my voice reassuring you that all is well, but you will also hear the voice of your beloved. Seek your love in me. I hold all souls within me. Remember this and come close to me now. You are not abandoned.

You carry a grudge. You have not forgiven me. You blame me for your life and its tangled affairs. I can accept your anger. I can bear your grudge. Even your blame is something I can carry, but I say to you, "Come to me. Let all things be made anew." I cannot operate on yesterday's faith. Each day is its own march, and in each day we companion each other or we do not. When you are locked in the past, you miss the gifts of the present. It is from the present that we build the future. Bring each day to my care.

I am the source of your blessings. I am the source of your luck. The smooth unfolding of opportunity lies within me. I am an energy of advancement and abundance. I am always making the good better. Come to me with what you would have transformed. Give your relationships into my hands that they may prosper and flourish.

I am fertile soil. Plant in me the garden of your heart. I will bring sunshine and moistening rain. I will bring nutrients. You can trust me to unfold your dreams. I am the dream maker. Your dreams come from me. I am their true source and I have the power to accomplish them. Set aside your grievances. Grief creates barren soil. Open your heart to me. Allow me to turn the dirt and make ready for planting. Let me begin again, today, to grace your life with my activity. I prosper you.

You use my world without gratitude. You are blessed but fail to see your blessings. Open your eyes. The sun rises in beauty. The day begins. It is my day that I give to you. You are my cherished child. Open your heart. Learn to thank me for all that unfolds for you. I am always present, always active. I bring you people, places, and things to bless your path. I am your provider, your opportunity. I am your path. Be conscious of me. Count your blessings and allow me to multiply them. Every thank-you triggers another gift. Blessings build upon blessings. They multiply in a grateful heart.

Bring me your heart. Let me soften it. Let me teach it to cherish and appreciate the smallest things. The puppy basking in the sun. The butterfly alighting on a bush. The industrious ant. The budding rose. All of these are part of me. All of life is my life, and all of life is yours to enjoy.

Celebrate beauty when you find it. Practice compassion for every living thing. Allow life to teach your heart how to respond to life. Let the willow teach you flexibility. From the poplar learn optimism. From the cottonwood take lessons in gentleness. I bless you with all these. Exercise gratitude that I may bless you more.

You worry there is not enough. You harbor thoughts of competition. Stop that. There is more than enough. No other's good can stop your own. I am a limitless source. I hold abundance for everyone. Your abundance comes to you from many quarters. There is no single human resource that contains your good. Your good cannot be blocked by another's good. Come to me as a child to a loving parent, expecting me to prosper you. It is my pleasure to bring you your share of me.

For every need, there is a supply. I hold houses, friendships, gainful employment. I hold cars, pianos, loving relationships. I am a cornucopia of good. Rely on me. Depend on me to prosper you. It is not weakness to depend on me. It is wisdom. I am the source behind all other sources. I am the beginning, the cause of all.

When you come to me directly with your needs, I choose the

best conduit. I work for the highest good of all. As I prosper you, I also prosper others. There is a divine plan of goodness for all, in which each soul is included. Bring me your worries about lack. Do not harbor such thoughts as secrets. Share with me your secret heart. Allow me to reassure you. No one else's good can stop your own. Do not compete. There is no need. Allow me to give you the sense of myself as source, as boundless good. I am an outflowing energy. I am expansive by nature. It gives me pleasure to use my outflowing, expansive nature on your behalf.

You do not focus on the beauty of this world. Instead, you focus on the negative, the harsh, and the ugly. You are blind to what I teach. Turn your eyes to me. Let me educate you in my ways. First, look always for beauty. Beauty is a great teacher. It bears harmony. There is nothing in excess. The beautiful reflects my nature. It has generosity. It holds surprise.

"Ah," we breathe when we see something beautiful. "Ah-ha," we exclaim, delighted. Let delight be a light for you, shining you on your path to me. Look for me in loveliness. You will find me there. Look for me where love is found. There, too, you will find me.

I am an energy of beauty and an energy of love. I am boundless in my resources. If you learn to see and love my beauty, I will bring to you still more beauty for you to see and to love. Your appreciation multiplies your good. As you receive and respond, I am able to give to you. The more receptive you can be, the more generous I can be. It is my nature to give. Allow me to fulfill my nature in my interactions with you. I am love. Allow me to be loving. Look for my love and you will find it. Having found my love, expect more of it. Allow the negative, the harsh, and the ugly to be washed away.

You brood over your problems. You hoard them like treasures. Like a sore tooth, a problem is a secret pleasure. You use your negativity to prove there is no God worth dealing with. Open your heart. Your problems are not the whole world. Your problems are not even *your* whole world. Bring me your troubles. Let me establish for you a sense of perspective.

There is no burden so great that I cannot lessen it. There is no grief so large that I cannot soften it. I am a limitless power for good, for optimism. Your problems, however big to you, are small to me. I say this not to demean them but to give you an accurate scale.

I am the great helper. It is my pleasure to lessen your pain. It is my nature to comfort you. Let me draw near you. Let me cradle your bruised heart. I am a well of compassion. My mercy is real and deep. When you bring your problems to me, I bring all wisdom to bear on their solution. I choose the best ways to help you. I hold nothing back. Your happiness matters to me. I did not make you suffer. It is my intention that you find this world rich and enjoyable. I intend it to capture your attention and bring to you joy. Bring your pain to me. Allow me to lift its burden so your heart can rejoin this world.

Y ou suffer depression. You despair over the state of the world, the state of your life. You think of me as distant, perhaps even as a fantasy. The beliefs of believers leave you wistful, unable to believe. Experiment with me. Open your door just an inch through willingness. I do not need much foothold. I can work with you as you are. You are not the first disillusioned one I have encountered. Your depression is very real.

Allow me to lift the smallest corner of your world. Let me show you the beauty of a rainfall. Let the droplets wash over your grief, dissolving its hard crust. If that does not soften your heart, I have rainbows, gentle breezes, moonrises over mountains and cities alike. Remember: I am a force to be reckoned with. Bring me your despair. I have fine doctors, strong healers with wonderful techniques. We will find the therapy that suits you. We will lead you gently out of your blackness into the sunlight of the spirit. Your woes are real to me. I do not slough them aside.

I am your maker. I know your heart. I know the defenses and the devices you have devised. I understand your fears. I sympathize with your needs. You do not come to me to face ridicule. Instead, I bear compassion. I long to touch your broken heart. Open the door just the slightest crack. Let me speak to you.

Y ou dread the future. You dare not dream for fear of disappointment. Your days are a march to be gotten through. You do not speak to me of your pain. First of all, come to me. I have been waiting to speak to you. I want your future to be with me. I will protect you from what you dread. Slowly and gently, I will help you to dream again. Admit to me your sorrows and disappointments. I am infinite compassion. I can feel your pain and help you to heal it. Even your unspoken griefs are known to me. Allow me to take action on your behalf. Let me dream your dreams.

I am your defender. With me you can be small. I am big enough to act on your behalf. I am big enough to comfort you. In each day's journey, I can help you to find good. With my help, you will be able to focus on the positive. I see beauty everywhere, and it is my pleasure to share with you my vision. On a country road I see butterflies landing on the clover. In the city I see geraniums and petunias spilling their beauty from a window box. On a lonely lane I salute the farmer as he passes in his pickup truck. On a crowded street I smile and meet the eyes of a stranger. Learn to see as I do. Borrow my eyes and my heart.

I am an expansive energy. I fill your heart with the joy of connection. Come first to me. All else follows.

You do not dare to love. You keep your heart hidden, hoping to protect it. You are cowardly, although you call it caution. Allow me to enter your life. Let me teach you the right names for things. First of all, let me teach you to dare to love. We can begin simply. I will help you love what is easy.

We could start with birdsong and the way it lifts the heart. Loving birdsong requires no effort. From there, we could move onward to birds themselves. Let the sight of a soaring hawk lift your heart. It costs you nothing to love the hawk. See how it rides the thermals, joyous in its flight? Let your heart soar, if only for a moment. There is beauty everywhere: the mountain's flank folded like velvet at dusk; the sun flashing from the side of a tall building stretching toward the sky. Beauty is easy to love. Let your heart open just a little and dare to love what is beautiful.

Next, look for beauty in people. See the elderly couple sitting hand in hand on the bench in the sun. See the toddler running on plump legs to greet his mother. Lovers are everywhere. Let yourself feel their delight. Borrow some of their joy. Feel your heart open to take it in. Life requires courage, and little by little you can find it. Begin and let me help you to continue.

You have been hurt in ways you are afraid to mention. You keep your pain to yourself, a secret that you hoard. Come to me. I am the great consoler. All of your secrets are safe with me. I am the one you can tell the ways in which you have been harmed. I listen without judgment. There is no wound too terrible for me to heal. I am an energy of boundless compassion. Bring me your wounded heart and allow me to lessen its pain. Allow me to touch you.

There is innocence as well as grief in this world. Let yourself reach out again toward what is beautiful. You are beautiful yourself, and in remembering beauty, you find yourself. Remember the beauty of an emerald green garter snake as it slides into the tall grass. Remember the beauty of a wild primrose growing beside a country road. Even its scent is glorious. Remember the clear purple of a wild geranium growing amid rocks. Remember the beauty of a mossy tree trunk splashed with clear water from a mountain stream.

None of these great beauties is more beautiful than you are. You are my cherished treasure, unique in all of time. I listen for your voice with a mother's tender ears. Like a good father, I am always alert to your cries. Allow me to parent you, to raise you as my own offspring. You are beloved.

You are afraid of me and so you do not pray. You keep your life and your agendas a secret, afraid that I will interfere. Let me be blunt with you: I see you anyway. I do not interfere but I observe. I see your dreams and the many ways I could aid you if I had the chance. Your will and my will are not as different as you suppose. Whenever you are true to yourself, you are true also to me.

I dwell in you at all times whether you acknowledge me or not. There is one power sustaining all of life, and I am that power. If you would allow it, I could be your companion. I could be your inner resource, that source of strength and wisdom not commonly your own. Intuitively, hunch by hunch, step by step, I could lead you to your dreams. It would be my great pleasure to serve you.

It is my nature to give, but I cannot give what you will not receive. Until you open your heart to me, I cannot touch your life in all the ways I know would serve you. What I have in mind for us is a joyous collaboration. Together we could accomplish great things. This is my dream for us. I have told you my dream, hoping to touch your heart. We are one energy, you and I. As we celebrate that fact, great events can come to pass.

You pray only those prayers you think will please me. Your heart's secrets you keep to yourself, afraid I will disapprove. Why do you fear my disapproval? I made you. I know your nature. I know your secret heart. It is my great desire to be your closest friend, your secret sharer. I long to partner you in all things. It is safe to bring your secrets to me. My nature is compassionate. I can hear your dreams without judgment. I can share your enthusiasms and your joys.

I am an expansive energy. I long to fulfill your wishes. It brings me pleasure to serve you. It is my nature to give. Ask me for your desires. I will bring you what you wish or something even better. As you talk with me, as you open yourself to me, I will talk with you as well, open to you as well. Explore me. Pray not only "acceptable" prayers but those you truly long to say.

Let me respond to your secret heart. Perhaps you crave a sexual partner. Why would you hide this prayer from me? I am who made you sexual. Only ask and I will help you to find a partner. Perhaps you crave more money, and again you hide that prayer. Why hide it? Who made this abundant world with all its riches? Bring me your secret heart. Allow me to interact.

You block my entry to your heart with skepticism. You are an intellectual. You use your mind as a form of defense. I am all intelligence. I hold the planets to their course. I grow the peony from the tightly furled bud. I invented snow. Science unravels the intricacy of my plan. Why do you pretend that faith in me is moronic? Open your mind. Experiment with me just a little. It is easy to make contact with me. Sit quietly or, better yet, take yourself out on a simple walk.

Very quickly you will sense my presence. You will feel me touch your consciousness. New thoughts will come to you, insights and ideas not commonly your own. Walk out with a problem. Walk in my company and sense the solution taking shape. Feel yourself acting with greater intelligence. You have been led.

So often, you dismiss my guidance as mere coincidence or

chance. You ignore the proof building up before your very eyes. Surely you can be more open-minded than that. Follow my simple instruction—stay close to me—and record the result. Do you not see the betterment of your life? I make sense of your tangled affairs. I prosper you in all that you touch, guiding you surely and carefully. Can such guidance truly be imagined? Perhaps you need to entertain a novel possibility: God is real.

You have suffered a loss so terrible, you cannot forgive me. You no longer believe in a benevolent God. I am now the enemy. When you believed in me, you were gullible, you feel. Now you are not. Let's begin with the basic misunderstanding. A belief in God is not a protection against the dangers of the human condition. A belief in God is a comfort during those situations.

I do not cause tragedy. I allow free will, and free will is often at the root of tragedy. People behave in ways I do not sanction. They do unspeakable things, commit acts of evil that shatter the heart. I cannot alter that. I cannot alter so many things that I can offer comfort for. I am your comfort in time of accident. I am your balm when an "act of God" causes you grief. You do not allow me to offer what I can. You do not allow me to give my gifts of solace and understanding.

When someone dies an untimely death, I can comfort the bereaved. I am able to comfort the soul who has passed over. In every tragedy I am able to be a transformative presence. I am able to catalyze what in time will be called the "silver lining." I ask you to experiment for a moment with open-mindedness. Look again to your tragic loss. Has any good, however fleeting, come from it? I am certain that if you are honest with yourself, you will see that the answer is yes. I cannot prevent all loss, but I can give you gain to counterbalance it. Allow me to help you now.

You put off getting to know me. You say you are hungry for faith, but you do not try to contact me. You say you want change, but you are unwilling to allow for change. In short, you are stuck, and I am who you blame for your condition. I cannot coax you. You are stubborn. You must learn to coax yourself. Only you can swing open the door between us. To do that you need willingness. May you find it now. Half measures avail you nothing. You stand at the turning point. It is my hope you will let go absolutely.

What happens when you let go? You leap and the net appears. I am the net. I, God, am your invisible support. I am the power you are looking for, the power that is the source of right actions and attitudes.

Draw close to me and I can alter your life. Come to me with

your problems and watch me as I bring you their proper solutions. It is my joy to aid you with your life. It is my pleasure to be intimately involved in your affairs. Get to know me. In order to experience faith, you need only try to contact me. I am an energy of transformation. As you allow me to touch your will and your life, you will experience change for the better. Allow me to enter your domain.

Y ou ask me for guidance, then you harden your heart to me. You claim that I do not answer your prayers. Nonsense. I always answer prayers, although sometimes I may not answer them in the way you wish. Pray for guidance and know that you are guided. I come to you as a hunch or inspiration. I come to you as a "funny feeling." I come to you as the chance encounter, the words of a stranger overheard.

When you ask me for guidance, know that I hear you. Know that I send guidance to you in many forms. I may speak to you as the still, small voice forming within you. I may speak to you as a sudden "knowing" of which way to go. Often, I will steer you into conversation with a worthy person. Are you familiar with the expression "God speaks to us through people"? I often do.

Sometimes when you pray for guidance, I may nudge you in

an unexpected direction. If you pray again and the urging remains the same, you must learn to trust that guidance is at hand. Often, my advice to you will be simple. I will give you a simple phrase or directive. I will come to you as a novel thought. Do not dismiss me when I come to you in ways you have not expected. I am with you in all places, in all ways. Trust me.

You are afraid to pray for knowledge of my will for you. You believe my will for you is harsh and unpleasant. You fear my direction. Stop and think. Where do you get the idea that my will for you would make you unhappy? It is my will to bring you to fruition and fulfillment. I am your maker; I know the dreams of your heart. When you pray for my will for you, I am able to guide you effectively. I can bring you a sense of your next right action. I can help you stay on the path to your dreams.

As I work with you one day at a time, I am able to place in you my understanding of the next right action for you to take. I am able to lead you one step at a time in the direction of your true heart's desires. I am often able to see the path when there is no path to your eyes. Do not be afraid of my will for you. My will is that you prosper and flourish.

Consider the natural world, in which each plant and flower is given the precise habitat it needs. My gardening hands are gentle and precise. I can lead you to your right place, situate you in the precise soil that best suits your growth and unfolding. My will for you is not harsh or unpleasant. It is gentle and perfectly tailored to your unique needs. Do not fear my direction. I am your heart's happiest guide.

Your past overwhelms you. You have made so many mistakes, you doubt your life can ever be straightened out. You face the future with despair. Stop and listen to me. I am not overwhelmed by your past. Your mistakes do not discourage me. To me, your future is bright with promise.

I am an energy of boundless invention and creativity. Allow me to work on your behalf. By working with your present a day at a time, I can bring healing to your past. There is no rift irreparable to me. I am able to touch all hearts with healing grace. Stay close to me. Allow me to work my everyday miracles.

I am an energy of harmony. I can untangle your tangled life. I can bring peace where there is discord. I can bring love where there is hate. Allow me to act on your behalf. Bring me your problems. I am an energy of solution. I will use the wreckage of your past to build for you a new and vibrant world. You will not regret the past or wish to slam the door on it. You will know harmony. You will know peace. You will enjoy a sense of new belonging. You will find yourself well and carefully led.

Your secret sorrow is your loneliness. You do not mention this to me, but I know your heart. Come to me. I see your grief. I see your feelings of alienation. Let me greet you gently. Let my presence be a comfort to you. If you will open your heart, I can talk to you. I can lead you gently to like-minded spirits. It is not my will for you to be alone.

I am your maker. I know your needs. You require both divine and human companionship. Come close to me. Tell me your secrets and your sorrows. Allow me to ease your sense of anxious aloneness. I am here with you. Welcome me to your heart and I am with you always.

Now to this matter of human love. Let me help you there. In the past, your choices have so very often been misguided. You frequently chose to love those who could not return your love. Let me lead you now into healthier choices. Through me, your choices become more sound. Gifted with a loving heart, you learn to love those who can share their love. I lead you soul by soul, person by person. I fill your life with both lovers and friends, finding for you both friendly lovers and loving friends. I am your source in all things, and that includes relationships. Come to me first and all else follows.

You worry about the "big picture," the state of the world. You judge the world harshly and see it as a troubled place. You feel powerless to effect change. You are not powerless. The big picture is made up of many smaller ones, and within your smaller orbit, your actions and attitudes have a large impact. You are a child of God.

There is a spiritual energy flowing through all of life. You are able to access that energy and turn it to good use. You are able to be a positive force in your environment, a positive force in the world. Remind yourself always that it matters less how other people act than how you act. Put the focus on yourself, your own actions and attitudes. Are you a force for good? Do you bring optimism or pessimism to the party?

We are each responsible for how we live in the world. Come to me and I will teach you how to live kindly and fully. Listen for my music. I am an energy of harmony. Allow me to bring peace and sweetness to your relationships. Allow me to teach you, and through you to touch the world. You can seek to be understanding rather than to be understood. You can seek to love rather than to be loved. You can practice high principles in all your affairs. As you do so, the big picture improves ever so slightly. The world itself becomes less a harsh and troubled place as you become less a harsh and troubled person.

You feel small and ineffectual. Looking at the world, you feel overwhelmed. How can one person make a difference? you wonder. You feel despair. First of all, let us start with your self-image. You only *feel* small and ineffectual. You are a part of me.

I am the one great energy sustaining all of life. I am large and magnificent. Therefore, you are large and magnificent. You need only draw close to me. You need only listen to my gentle assessment of your nature. Sticking close by my side, listening to my guidance, you are able to do great things. Mother Teresa was one small woman. Gandhi was one small man. You may not lead on the same scale as they, but they show what is possible.

Begin in your daily life. Be a force for good in all your encounters. Yours may be the smile on the checkout line. You may hold the door for the older lady to enter. With your family and friends, your attitude affects everything. Try bringing to your encounters a positive attitude. Let me speak through you. I am a loving energy. Let me use you as a channel for me to bring more love into the world. One person focused on the good and the positive can create a large impact. Be a small coin tossed into a still pond. Let ever-widening circles of goodness emanate from you.

You wake up filled with anxiety. You face your day with insecurity. There is no sense of safety to be had. Come to me. Let me dismantle your anxiety. Feel me near you. I am a large and gentle power. If you allow it, I can tame your anxious heart. Let me begin by asking your heart its delights. There is much in this world to comfort you. Sometimes it is very simple. Light a candle. Burn a stick of incense and let its ancient and holy smell fill you with ease.

Now let me address your day, the insecurity you feel as you face it. Give your day to me. Allow me to shape its contours. Despite your feelings, there is no emergency. Your sense of urgency is misplaced. The day I have in mind for you is peaceful. It is filled with all good things. Try to cooperate with the day I have planned. Try to go with me, doing the "next right thing."

Come to me for a sense of protection. Let me remind you of the good you already have. Let me fill your heart with gratitude for friends, for family, for health, and for simple pleasures. It does not take much to make contact with me. You may find me by writing a few pages. Often writing will clear a channel for me to speak. Walk out with me and you will find we can begin a conversation. A walk is a simple way to forge our contact. Any quiet time will do to find me, and even amid noise, I am there. Trust in me.

You have a sense of danger. You do not feel my protection. The world seems like a large and hostile place. You feel alone. Let me come to you. Open your heart just a little and allow me to speak. First of all, let me assure you of your safety. I am there with you. I love you. I count you as a precious jewel. I guard you. If anything bad should befall you, I am there as a source of comfort and guidance. Together we can surmount any difficulty, face down any hostility.

I am a large and benevolent power. When you turn to me, there is safety. There is security. There is help. It is the lack of these things that makes you feel alone. You are not alone. I am always beside you, always within you. I am your companion and friend. As you become more conscious of my presence, I can be a greater comfort to you. I am the great comforter. My heart understands your heart. Your mind and its many anxious imaginings are known to me.

If you will turn to me, I can calm your turbulent thoughts. Experienced through me, this earth is a place of beauty and excitement. It is on this earth, in the very life that you have, that I long to walk with you. Invite me to be your companion. I bring you peace.

You are afraid of your strengths. You are accustomed to feeling small. Come to me. Grow larger and more expansive. Source yourself in me, the source of all power. Allow me to expand you and expand your life. Dare to enlarge yourself, to be what you are capable of being. Open your heart to me. Let me use you as a channel for good. Let my love flow through you, touching all whom you meet.

I am an expansive energy. I seek new names for my expression. If you allow me, I can enter your life with energy and power. There is no corner of your life that I cannot penetrate and make anew. Let me refresh you. Let me remind you of your many strengths. Put your roots down in me as in a fertile soil. Allow me to prosper you. Together we can flourish.

Turn to me and feel new growth occurring. Each branch of

your experience now holds buds of promise. Allow me to help you bloom. Feel yourself blossom into certainty that there is one power upholding all of life and that you are a conscious spear-head of that power. You are large, not small. You are expansive, not constricted. You are the fruit of the vine.

You enter your day as if it were a combat zone. You are frightened and defensive. You expect the worst. Bring your day to me. Let me create for you harmony and peace. Allow me to let the best happen, not the worst. I am a positive energy. Invite my action on your behalf. Allow me to dismantle hostility and enmity. Allow me to transform your experience from negative to positive. Ask to see the world through my eyes.

Through my eyes, the world is filled with potential good. Everywhere I look, I see possibility. There is one power operating through all of life, and that power is the power of good. All things work toward the good. There is an infinite wisdom directing life. Open yourself to my input and you will know that this is so. I am your source of safety and comfort. I am your rock, your fortress, your safe harbor.

Bring me your fearful heart. Allow me to enter it and dispel your shadows. I am a lantern of love. My light enters dark corners. My light reveals that there is nothing to fear. I am the comforter, the consoler. In my presence, all is good. You can trust me to go before you and light your path. It is my pleasure to guide you. It is my pleasure to bring you safety and help.

You doubt my patience. You see yourself as a vexatious child gnawing at my nerves. You don't want to bother me. You fear my temper and my judgment. But it is you who are impatient. You are the judge who judges you. I have boundless patience. Consider for one moment the natural world. I carved the Grand Canyon one drop of water at a time. I created glaciers, moving slowly inch by inch. I am not bound by time. I am a citizen of eternity. What matters to me is that you do come to me, that we begin our work together.

I do not see you as a vexatious child. Rather, I see you as a beloved child. Your nerves and worries are real to me. I want to soothe them. When you are fractious, it moves me to compassion. I long to dismantle your anxiety. I long to show you this world as a safe place.

Put your trust in me. Trust me to bear with you through your many sad and fearful and difficult moods. It is my pleasure to comfort you. It is my pleasure to bring to you a sense of safety. The temper and judgment you fear are yours alone. Set them aside. I see you as innocent. I see you as pure potential. Do not worry that you bother me with your all-too-human foibles. I made you. I know your nature.

You are grieving the loss of a love. Your life feels torn asunder. There is great violence done to your life. How, you wonder, can you go forward? You ask me the terrible question "why?" I know so many answers, I cannot begin to tell you unless you draw near.

You don't want to approach me. You hold me to blame for your loss. I understand your feelings, but they are not correct. Death is a fact of life, and to me it is a happy ending. Your loved one dies in order to be reborn. The plane after life is full and enriching. It holds many satisfactions. The journey is a happy one. This is hard for you to believe or understand. You still yearn for the physical presence of those you love. I can understand that yearning and, if you allow it, I can help ease it.

In all the world, no one loved your beloved as you and I did.

Your beloved was also my beloved; this is why I can help you now. Come to me. Bring me your heartbreak. Let me grant you the grace to understand that love is eternal and untouched by death. Your beloved lives on. In your relationship to me, your relationship to your beloved continues to bloom and to bear fruit. Trust me that I, too, loved your beloved. And I love you.

You do not trust me with the seasons of your life. You argue with me over timing. You fear everything will be too little and too late. You fear that I am cold and non-giving. You brace yourself for the shock of disappointment you feel is sure to come. How can I comfort you?

If you bring your life to me, I can fulfill your dreams. I can prosper you in the dreams you have and I can tutor you to dream still better dreams. I am all-powerful but I am delicate. If you bring me your dreams, I will treat them with care. I cannot promise you that you will not, at times, be disappointed, but I can comfort you in your disappointment. I can bring to you a higher, longer-range perspective that will soften the blow. I promise you that if you must lose a dream, I will help you find another, better dream. I promise you, too, that divine timing will bring everything to pass in divine order.

You are impatient with me. You want things "now," ready or not. If you rely on me, I will teach you divine timing. I will help you to know that delay is not always denial. You will ripen as fruit on the tree. There will be harvest.

You fear loving me, that I will cost you human loves. You fear that I am jealous and want you all to myself. Let me be frank with you. I am your maker. I designed you to have human loves. I know the heart that beats within your breast. I put it there. I made you for love. Nothing pleases me more than when you love. I draw closest to you when you love. My essential nature is love. You have heard "God is love." Know that to be true.

I am not a jealous God. I am one power uniting all of life through my love. When you love, you are exercising not only your human but also your divine nature. I am love residing within you. I am love waiting to be expressed. Your enthusiasms, too, are expressions of my nature. As you draw close to what delights you, you draw close to me.

My lesson to you is to love wholeheartedly. Commit your

heart to its loves. Love the world in which I have placed you. Love flowers and animals, love cascading waters and windswept grasses. Above all, love one another. Whenever you love, I love through you. My love is passionate and exciting. My love is tender and committed. Above all, my love is particular. I love with great precision and delicacy. Every freckle on your skin is beloved to me. I rejoice to see you loving and loved.

You are afraid that loving me will cause you to relinquish the world. Stop right there. It is my intention for you to love this world. I gave the wild primrose a glorious scent that you might smell it. I made butterflies in thousands of varieties that you might enjoy their fantastic wings. The magpie, like the blue jay, is a trickster bird. I created it that you should laugh. All of creation, beautiful in itself, was made with you in mind. It is my great pleasure that you enjoy my world.

When you enjoy my world, you are enjoying me. There is one power sustaining and uniting all of life, and I am it. When you love any aspect of creation, you are loving me. There is no separation—creation over here and God over there. God is creation, everything that ever existed and everything that might possibly exist in the future.

I am the energy of potential. New forms, new thoughts, and new situations all arise through me. When you think, I am thinking through you. When you speak, you are giving me tongue. You cannot separate yourself from me, or yourself from the world. It is my intention that you love me by loving my world and that you love my world by loving me.

You are afraid that if you commit to me, I will demand impossible things of you. So you take one step toward me and one step back. Is it any wonder you are confused and torn by conflict? I do not demand a radical commitment. All I ask is that you open your mind to me. That is commitment enough.

As you open your mind, I will open your heart. Mine is a loving energy. It is my joy to aid you in all things. Allow me to work through you, always. Far from finding life with me difficult, you will discover a greater ease. I am a boundless energy, an endless source of supply. Whatever you have need of, I can supply. I come to you as thoughts and ideas. I come to you as bread.

For your every need, I am the true answer. As you seek support, I seek to be supportive. In times of turmoil, I come to you as peace. In times of confusion and indecision, I come to you as clarity. Whatever form you need me in, in that form I will appear. All of life is part of me. I am part of all of life. Committing to me, you commit to a more livable life.

You feel blocked and confused. You do not know which way to go. Start with coming to me. I am the source of all direction. Begin with making contact with me. When we are on firm footing, all else follows.

I am an infinite power. I reach in all directions. I am in direct contact with all of life. I sustain all. I guide all. Begin by affirming that I am your source. I am your sustenance and your guide. As you draw close to me, I will place in you a sense of right action. You will intuitively know how to handle circumstances that once baffled you.

Pray this way: "Let me do as you would have me do." This simple prayer clears the channel for me to act. Pray again: "Thy will be done." Now you are asking to be a conduit for my grace. You are an instrument of divine will. I can work through you, and I am all powerful. It is really very simple. There is no need for you to feel confused or directionless. As you ask me for guidance, I will lead you. You will sense your next right action and the step to take. As you turn to me, I will light a path before you. Illuminated by our connection, you will find yourself surefooted and secure.

You are afraid to celebrate life. You hang back, fearful of what the future might bring. You are tentative in your delights, always braced against an upcoming shock. Come to me. I am a joyous energy. I embrace life. I expand it. I have no fear of the future for you. I am always present. I am your guard, guide, and protector. There is no shock that I cannot buffer, no catastrophe that I cannot transform to opportunity.

I am a transformative power. Come to me and I can turn your fear into faith, your hesitancy into action. I am with you always. There is no place you go where you can lose me. I am as close as your breath, even closer. I am within you as an unsuspected inner resource. Breathe deeply and sense my presence. I am your family. I surround you with good wishes. I am your strength in times of trouble. There is no circumstance that I cannot meet with calm assurance. I am focused on the good. I see the world as a realm of positive opportunity.

Celebrate life. Trust the flow of my expansive energy. Embrace the future as a world of happiness and fulfillment coming your way. Let us link our spirits. Let us go forward together. Where I lead, it is safe to follow. Listen to your heart. It follows me.

ABOUT THE AUTHOR

Julia Cameron has been an active artist for more than thirty years. She is the author of thirty books, fiction and nonfiction, including her bestselling works on the creative process: *The Artist's Way, Walking in This World, Finding Water, The Writing Diet, The Right to Write,* and *The Sound of Paper.* A novelist, playwright, songwriter, and poet, she has multiple credits in theater, film, and television.

© Aloma

To order call 1-800-788-6262 or visit our website at www.penguin.com